D0118480

you are what you eat™
you are
what
you eat

the **meal planner** that
will **change your life**

Compiled by Carina Norris, MSc Public Health Nutrition

celador
international
LICENSING

Acknowledgements

Virgin Books and Celador International would like to extend a big thank you to the following for their assistance in compiling this book at record speed: all those *You Are What You Eat* participants who kindly agreed to feature as case studies in the book; Justine Pattison for her contribution to the recipes; Roz Denny and Beverly Le Blanc for writing additional recipes; and Dan Newman at Perfect Bound for designing the book. A special thanks to the *You Are What You Eat* production team, especially Damon Pattison, Charlotte Reid and Yvette Dore, and also to Rosanna Arciuli and Amanda Lightstone at Celador International.

Carina Norris, MSc (Dist) Public Health Nutrition, is an accomplished magazine editor, journalist and health writer, with a particular interest in making healthy eating understandable, practical, and enjoyable for all.

First published in Great Britain in 2006 by
Virgin Books Ltd
Thames Wharf Studios
Rainville Road
London
W6 9HA

A catalogue record for this book is available from the British Library.

This edition produced for
The Book People Ltd, Hall Wood Avenue, Haydock, St Helens, WA11 9UL

ISBN 0 7535 1137 1

The paper used in this book is a natural, recyclable product made from wood grown in sustainable forests. The manufacturing process conforms to the regulations of the country of origin.

Designed by Dan Newman, Perfect Bound Ltd
Printed and bound in Great Britain by Bath Press

Every effort has been made to ensure that the information in this book is accurate. The information in this book will be relevant to the majority of people but may not be applicable in each individual case so it is advised that professional medical advice is obtained for specific information on personal health matters. Neither the publisher nor Celador accept any legal responsibility for any personal injury or other damage or loss arising from the use or misuse of the information and advice in this book. Anyone making a change in their diet should consult their GP especially if pregnant, infirm, elderly or under 16.

Recipe shots courtesy of Salton Europe/Russell Hobbs/John Norbury.
Food tables courtesy of Celador Productions.
Lifestyle and general food shots courtesy of Corbis.

contents

foreword

The idea for the *You Are What You Eat* TV show came about in the summer of 2003. It seemed that every day nutrition and obesity were headline news and more and more people were making the link between what we eat and how we feel. In short, if we eat rubbish, we will probably feel pretty rubbish too.

We wanted to turn this growing awareness into a TV show and we thought that the best way to do it would be to tackle the worst eaters in Britain. We needed to find really unhealthy people who gorged themselves on nothing but junk food. Then we could demonstrate how their appalling lifestyle was affecting their health. We had the premise for the show; all we needed now was the title. We thought about using *Eat Fast, Die Young*, *Hate Your Guts* or *Get Stuffed*, but eventually settled on *You Are What You Eat*. It seemed like a straightforward title that epitomised the show's message: eat badly, feel bad; eat well, feel better. Simple.

When the show went on air, it immediately grabbed people's attention and quickly became 'must see' TV. The success of the series also helped us to create two bestselling books.

We're now on series three of the TV show and this is the third book. However, the message remains the same: eating healthily can have a really positive effect on the way you feel and look. Any change in your eating habits, no matter how small, will help you reap the benefits of a healthy lifestyle.

The third *You Are What You Eat* book is crammed with all the good advice of the TV show. There's also a simple meal planner to help you make sensible food choices throughout the year and tips aimed at families tackling the nightmare of getting children to try something different which – shock horror – might just be good for them! In addition there are lots of helpful hints, suggestions and recipes for year-round eating to encourage long-term change.

But the point is you don't have to do it all at once and you don't have to do it all the time – just have a go and see how you feel. You might be amazed.

Good luck!

Damon Pattison
Head of Entertainment Development, Celador Productions

introduction

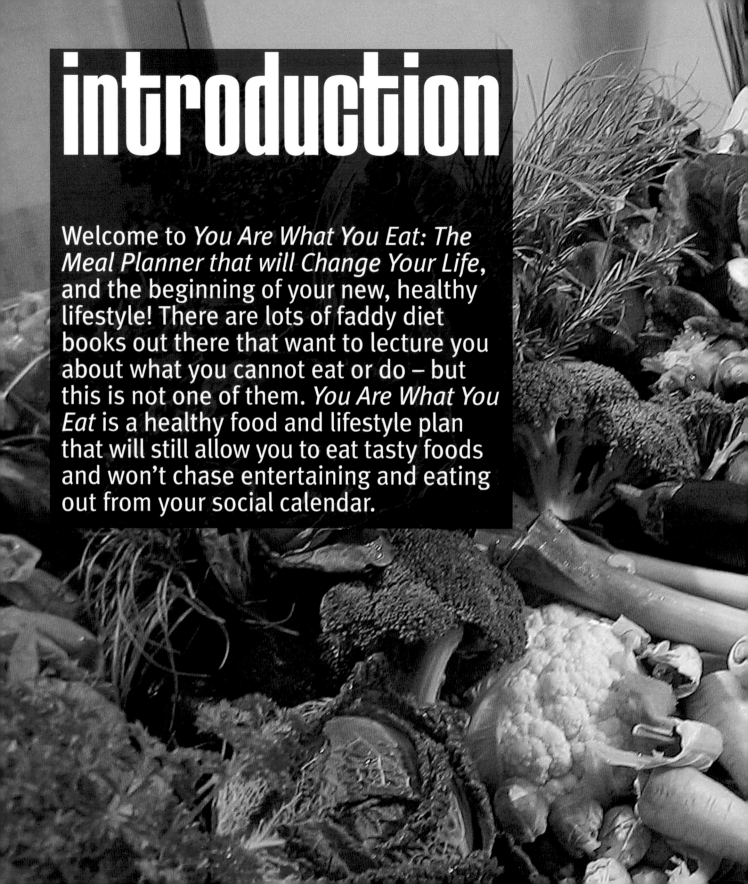

Welcome to *You Are What You Eat: The Meal Planner that will Change Your Life*, and the beginning of your new, healthy lifestyle! There are lots of faddy diet books out there that want to lecture you about what you cannot eat or do – but this is not one of them. *You Are What You Eat* is a healthy food and lifestyle plan that will still allow you to eat tasty foods and won't chase entertaining and eating out from your social calendar.

Here's what you'll find inside this book:

- The knowledge to understand the dramatic effects your food has on your body, your health, and your happiness
- The means to understand why you eat what you eat, helping you to spot the triggers that may cause you to make unhealthy food choices
- The nutritional know-how to make healthy food choices
- Meal plans and over a hundred nutritious recipes, to give you a fantastic healthy repertoire of food for your family and friends
- Practical lifestyle 'Actions' to help you get moving and motivated, and also relaxed and restored
- Lots of practical tips and useful quizzes to help you adopt a new, healthy lifestyle

For every month of the year, there's helpful, practical nutritional advice on important food themes, plus that all-important 'Action' to link your new way of eating to the activity in the rest of your life. The themes aren't tied to the particular months, but many of them are timely, such as good resolutions in the New Year, making the most of the fabulous fresh fruit and vegetables available seasonally, and enjoying the festive season – the healthy way.

The first section of this book will give you a good idea of what *You Are What You Eat* is all about, and set you on your way to a new, happier and healthier lifestyle. Or you may wish to skip ahead to something that particularly interests you, such as activities for children, or lunchboxes for grownups. Feel free – this is a book that you can dip into and refer to again and again.

You live in the real world, with all the pressures of work, family and relationships. You know that mornings are always a rush, that children seem to have an instinctive distrust of new foods, that the family budget can't always stretch as far as you'd like, and that you never have time for exercise. So this book won't tell you to do anything that's impossible.

It will simply show you how you can regain control of your eating, and your life!

So you've decided you want to take control of your eating and enjoy the rewards of a healthy diet! Good for you!

Rather than embarking on a strict, formulaic diet, you're setting off on a journey towards a whole new way of eating. By changing the kinds of foods you eat – cutting out the fatty, sugary, processed junk, and replacing it with tasty, fresh wholefoods – you'll be giving your body the fuel it needs, rather than the rubbish that clogs it up and slows it down. And your body will reward you with increased energy levels, clearer skin, shinier hair, better circulation, fewer minor illnesses and improved all-round health. You could also add years to your life – eating healthily reduces your risk of the big killer diseases such as cancer, heart disease and stroke.

But diet is only part of the picture – to complete the whole, you'll need to add exercise and relaxation. Physical activity plays a vital role in supporting our immune systems, keeping our cholesterol levels in check, maintaining a healthy weight, keeping our muscles (including our hearts) strong and toned, building and maintaining healthy bones, and balancing stress hormones.

And exercise isn't just for the body – it also helps your mind. Exercise stimulates the production of endorphins, the 'happy' chemicals produced by the body that make you feel exhilarated and motivated. So exercise is not only good for you . . . it makes you feel happy, and that can't be bad.

This book isn't a weight-loss diet, but if you need to lose weight, and were eating badly before, the pounds will fall away. You won't be eating less food, just better food. And the healthier foods will sustain you between meals so you won't need that mid-morning chocolate biscuit! Combine this with a healthy amount of exercise, and your body will stabilise at the natural, healthy weight for you.

For now, all you need are a few guidelines. Follow these, and you'll soon be eating healthily. Add the exercise, and everything will fall into place. They may look daunting – but don't panic! Even if you start by changing just one bad food habit, you're on your way. Do as much as you can, and don't worry if you're taking baby steps, not giant leaps. But as soon as you begin feeling the benefits of your new healthy lifestyle, your motivation will soar.

You could add years to your life – eating healthily reduces your risk of the big killer diseases such as cancer, heart disease and stroke.

THE *YOU ARE WHAT YOU EAT*
10 STEPS TO A HEALTHIER LIFESTYLE

1   Eat breakfast

2   Get the hydration habit – and drink plenty of water

3   Cut down on caffeine

4   Get fresh – eat plenty of fresh food

5   Eat Five-a-day – fruit and vegetables

6   Banish the frying pan – use low-fat cooking methods

7   Eat good fats – top up your polyunsaturates

8   Make it yourself – don't rely on processed food

9   Cut down on sugar and salt

10   Finger on the pulse – eat more beans, lentils and wholegrain foods

1 EAT BREAKFAST

The importance of breakfast cannot be overemphasised. Skip breakfast, and by mid-morning you'll feel sluggish and irritable. Perhaps this is normal for you, but it's not a nice feeling, is it? Maybe you kick-start your body with a cup of coffee instead of breakfast, but that's not a good idea either.

A filling, nourishing breakfast sets you up for the day, sustaining your energy levels through the morning, and giving you the self-control to resist the muffins and biscuits that seem to go so well with elevenses, but leave you craving more soon afterwards.

Sugary breakfast cereals aren't the answer. They'll give your blood-sugar levels an instant boost, but it won't last. Far better to fuel up with slow release fuels like cereals with no added sugar – if you miss the sweetness, add some chopped fresh or tinned fruit. Use skimmed or semi-skimmed milk (both good sources of protein and calcium) rather than full fat and you'll cut the fat content of your breakfast, too.

What about croissants? Sorry – croissants are packed with butter, and full of unhealthy saturated fats. Wholemeal toast, though, is a good source of slow-release complex carbohydrate, and better than white bread, from which a lot of the nutrients and fibre have been removed. But go easy on the spread!

Protein is another secret weapon against the mid-morning nibbles! Adding protein to your breakfast increases the time until you'll feel hungry again.

Pep up your breakfast with protein:
- Add natural yogurt to your cereal or muesli
- Sprinkle some chopped nuts and seeds on your cereal – try walnuts, almonds, Brazil nuts, hazelnuts, flaxseeds, pumpkin seeds, sunflower seeds or sesame seeds.
- Top your wholemeal toast with no-sugar baked beans or a poached or scrambled egg.

> Scientists have found that children who eat a good breakfast do better in school – their concentration span increases and they are less likely to be distracted.

2 GET THE HYDRATION HABIT

Your body contains approximately 65 per cent water, and it's vital to keep hydrated. People can survive for six weeks without food, but only a few days with no water. Even mild dehydration can make you feel weak, dizzy and lacking in energy.

You need to drink approximately 1.5–2 litres of water a day: that's about 8–10 glasses. If you buy a large bottle of mineral water and keep topping up your glass throughout the day, it will help you to keep track of the amount you're drinking. If you're not used to drinking a lot of water, build up to your target gradually.

Your fluid needs

Sometimes you will need more water than usual. The following will increase the amount of water lost from your body, requiring it to be replenished:

- Strenuous work or exercise
- Hot temperatures
- Heated or recirculated air (as in offices or aeroplanes)
- Pregnancy and breastfeeding – both increase a woman's need for fluids
- Fever, diarrhoea and vomiting

Caffeine on your mind

Caffeine is a behaviour-modifying drug! It stimulates the central nervous system, blocking a natural sedative produced by the brain (making us feel more alert), and causes the heart to beat faster.

But our attachment to caffeine is also psychological. Look at the list of caffeine-containing food and drink in the box, and you'll see how many of them have pleasurable, warm and fuzzy associations. A mug of cappuccino with a friend, wrapping your hands around a steaming mug of hot chocolate, or the chocolates you buy yourself as a treat. It isn't just the caffeine in coffee and chocolate that makes us feel good!

Although pure water is by far the best fluid to keep you hydrated, you can also boost your fluid intake with herbal and fruit teas and diluted fruit juice. Fizzy drinks are packed with sugar and are bad for your teeth, and squash is generally the same. But if you simply can't give up sweet drinks straightaway, choose a good-quality fruit juice and add water, gradually making it weaker and weaker, until you've weaned yourself onto pure water.

Tea and (especially) coffee are diuretics and stimulants, so try to minimise your intake. Alcohol should only be drunk in moderation, and should not count towards your fluid intake!

3 CUT DOWN ON CAFFEINE

Many of us love our coffee. It gives us a kick-start in the morning, and keeps us going when we're feeling drowsy. It gives us a buzz, and makes us feel alert and happy.

Coffee, and caffeine-containing food and drinks, have a stimulant effect, but this isn't always a good thing. We can grow used to the 'caffeinated feeling' so that anything else feels sluggish, so we keep reaching for the coffee to keep the buzz. Some people are sensitive to caffeine, and even a couple of cups of coffee a day can make their hearts race, and they feel jittery and anxious. Pregnant women also need to be careful about their caffeine intake.

Try low-caffeine or caffeine-free alternatives to coffee and tea – there's a wide variety available. They won't taste exactly the same, but it's not too difficult to persuade yourself that they can fill the coffee- or tea-shaped hole in your day. Try instant-coffee substitutes made from dried chicory, barley, figs or dandelion root, and herbal teas instead of your regular cuppa. Rooibos, or Redbush tea, is another delicious alternative. And if you prefer a sweeter taste, try fruit teas.

Caffeine counter

It's not only in the coffee cup that you'll find caffeine lurking:

SOURCE	CAFFEINE CONTENT
Mug of instant coffee	100 mg
Cup of brewed coffee	100 mg
Can of energy drink	up to 80 mg
Cup of instant coffee	75 mg
Cup of tea	50 mg
Chocolate bar (50g)	50 mg
Can of cola	up to 40 mg
Cup of hot chocolate	5mg
Cup of decaffeinated coffee	3mg

Many painkillers and cold cures also contain caffeine, so check the label.

4 GET FRESH!

The fresher your food, the more nutrients it will contain. The minute they're picked or pulled out of the ground, the vitamin content of fruit and vegetables begins to decline. So it's better, if you can, to shop for fresh food little and often.

It pays to look for home-grown fruit and vegetables when they are in season and to take advantage of pick-your-own growers, farm shops and farmers' markets.

Check the sell-by dates on packaged fruit and vegetables and try to buy and use as far before the dates as you can.

If you buy organic, you'll get fewer chemicals such as pesticides on fruit and vegetables, and fewer hormones, antibiotics and growth-promoters in meat, milk and eggs, so organic food is good for minimising the amount of potentially nasty substances your body has to detoxify.

Fresh, frozen or canned?

There's no denying that fresh fruit and vegetables, in their natural state and straight from the ground or tree, are best for you.

But just how fresh is fresh? The produce you see in the supermarket could have been harvested several weeks ago, and their vitamin contents will have declined.

Frozen foods, on the other hand, are flash-frozen soon after harvesting, which means that the vitamin loss is negligible.

Before being canned, fruit and vegetables are thoroughly boiled, which means that much of their water-soluble B vitamins and vitamin C can be lost. Canned fruits may be canned in sugary syrup, and canned vegetables often have added salt and sugar.

In summary, while fresh or frozen is generally best, canned fruit and vegetables are better than none at all, and may contain more nutrients than old, wizened 'fresh' produce.

Organic essentials

If you can only afford to buy a few organic products, put these at the top of your list:

Apples

Peppers

Celery

Grapes

Nectarines and peaches

Pears

Potatoes

Spinach

If you have the space and 'green fingers', try growing your own herbs, vegetables and salads – it really is satisfying.

5 EAT FIVE-A-DAY

The World Health Organisation says we should all be eating at least five portions of fruit and vegetables a day – and with good reason. Fruit and veg are rich in essential vitamins and minerals, fibre, carbohydrates, and beneficial phytochemicals. They've also been linked to many health benefits, including lowered risk for certain cancers, stroke, heart disease, and high blood pressure. And if five-a-day is good, more is even better!

Potatoes, although a good source of carbohydrate, do not count towards your five-a-day. You should get your five or more from fresh, tinned or frozen fruit and vegetables. You can also include one portion of fruit juice (a small glass), or a portion of dried fruit (1/2–1 tablespoon) towards your total.

The exceptional tomato

Tomatoes are packed with vitamins and minerals, including the powerful antioxidant lycopene, which also helps protect against prostate cancer.

Most fruit and vegetables lose nutrients when they're cooked, but tomatoes are the exception to the rule. Canned tomatoes are actually more nutritious than their fresh cousins – cooking them during the canning process makes it easier for the body to use the beneficial compounds inside them.

6 BAN THE FRYING PAN

And send the deep-fat fryer packing! Fried food soaks up oil, and can bump up your fat intake to astronomical proportions.

From now on, you should avoid frying food wherever possible. When you do fry, you should use olive, corn, sunflower or rapeseed oil, and use only a tiny quantity for a short amount of time, as in stir-frying.

For a healthier lifestyle put away the frying pan and use other cooking methods:

- Poaching: Poaching in water or stock requires no fat. Ideal for vegetables, chicken, fish and eggs.
- Grilling: Allows the fat in poultry, fish and meat to run off.
- Stewing: Ideal for slow cooking of less tender cuts of meat. Remove the fat from the meat before browning in a dry pan, then add your stock.
- Stir-frying: A quick spray of a good-quality oil is all that is needed.
- Steaming: No oil is needed. Steaming is a great way to retain the vitamins and minerals when cooking vegetables. When you boil food, you lose a lot of the water-soluble vitamins (the B vitamins and vitamin C) into the cooking water.
- Baked 'parcels': Bake vegetables, skinned boneless chicken and fish in greaseproof-paper parcels.
- Roasting: Remove excess fat from meat, and skin from poultry, before roasting on a rack in a nonstick roaster.
- Griddling: Ideal for meat and poultry as it allows the oil to drain off.

7 EAT GOOD FATS

Not all fats are bad!

Good fats, bad fats

All fats are high in calories, so will cause weight gain if you eat too much of them. But monounsaturated fats and polyunsaturated fats have health benefits, and our bodies suffer when we're lacking in them.

The problem is, our diets are generally much higher in the 'bad' saturated fats than the good fats. We need to cut down on the baddies, while ensuring we have enough of the health-promoting fats.

Know your enemies – and your friends

Saturated fats: These are the kind that raise your cholesterol levels, cause atherosclerosis ('clogging' of the arteries), and increase your risk of heart disease. They're generally solid at room temperature, and are found in animal products (meat, eggs, dairy products) and 'tropical oils' such as coconut and palm oil.

Trans fats: Trans fats are also known as hydrogenated vegetable oils, and have undergone a hardening process to improve their keeping products. These fats have similar harmful effects to saturated fats – in fact, they may be even worse for us.

Two kinds of cholesterol – friend and foe

Cholesterol is bad - right? Well, yes and no. There are two kinds of cholesterol, and one of them is actually good for you!

The cholesterol we want to avoid is called LDL cholesterol. Eating saturated and trans fats increases our blood levels of this 'bad' cholesterol, which clogs our arteries and increases our risk of heart disease.

The other cholesterol is called HDL cholesterol, and this 'good' cholesterol reduces our risk of heart disease. Eating saturated and trans fats lowers our levels of beneficial HDL cholesterol, while eating monounsaturated and polyunsaturated fats raises it.

These fats sneak into a huge range of processed foods, to lengthen their shelf life – yet another reason to cook your own!

Monounsaturated fats: Olive oil, canola oil and peanut oil, and also avocados, are high in monounsaturates. Olive and canola oils (in small quantities, of course) are the best oils for frying, as they are less susceptible to being damaged by heat and forming harmful compounds that can damage our bodies.

Polyunsaturated fats: Safflower oil, sunflower oil and corn oil are all good sources of polyunsaturates. Omega-3 and omega-6 fatty acids are polyunsaturates: found in oily fish, nuts and seeds, they help lower our cholesterol levels, reduce our risk of heart disease, and even benefit our mood.

8 MAKE IT YOURSELF

Give up your processed-food habit! Processed foods are generally packed with salt, sugar and saturated and trans fats – all nutritional baddies. They're also often loaded with bulkers, fillers and additives, with no nutritional value.

If you prepare and cook your own food from scratch, you'll know exactly what went into it. You'll find plenty of useful tips, ideas and recipes in this book to ease you into home cooking without spending hours in the kitchen.

9 CUT DOWN ON SUGAR AND SALT

It's a fact that most of us eat far too much sugar and salt. Sugary foods can contribute to obesity and tooth decay, as well as crowding out more nutritious foods from our diets. Sugar gives us instant energy, but the feeling doesn't last, and in no time at all we're hungry again and craving more sweet things.

Although the body needs sugars as a fuel, it's perfectly capable of getting them from the natural sugars in fruits, and by breaking down starchy carbohydrates and even protein and fats. And while the sugar in sweets, biscuits and other sugary processed food has little to recommend it, fruits and starchy carbohydrates (especially 'complex' carbohydrates in wholemeal foods, oats, and pulses such as lentils and beans) have a whole host of health benefits.

Swap your sugary snack for a piece of fruit, a handful of dried fruit, or a wholemeal currant bun or scone. And revamp your dessert repertoire to fill it with delicious alternatives that are lower in sugar – you'll find plenty of inspiration in this book.

Salt can contribute to high blood pressure, increasing our risk of heart disease and stroke. Many of us have too much, especially if we eat a lot of processed foods. Wean yourself off adding salt at the table (taste your food first – you'll be surprised at how often it doesn't need extra salt), add less in cooking, and cut down the amount of processed foods you serve.

What spread?

Do you need something to spread on your toast or sandwiches? Look at the label and go for a spread that's high in polyunsaturates and low in saturates. If it says 'low in trans fats', that's good too. Also look at the ingredients list and try to avoid hydrogenated fats, hydrogenated vegetable oil, partially hydrogenated vegetable oil and palm oil. You probably won't be able to avoid them all, but it helps to know that the ingredients that come first in the list are those that the product contains the most of.

Listen to your stomach

Our bodies have a remarkably effective system for telling us when we've eaten enough – the problem is, we're all too good at over-riding it.

Cues such as the amount and type of food in our stomachs, our blood-sugar levels and the levels of other nutrients in the blood, send messages to our brains, telling us that it's time to stop eating now.

But we can override these messages – think how easy it is, when you're already full up, to say, 'Oh, maybe just a little slice' when the dessert arrives!

And, all too often, we eat for the wrong reasons – because it's a food we like, because we're feeling bored or upset, or because it's being offered by someone we care about.

Eating quickly can also lead to eating too much. It can take up to half an hour for the stomach to 'recognise' that it's had enough (depending on the type of food eaten), so eat slowly, concentrating on your meal. Learn to recognise the 'full' feeling, and don't be afraid to leave food on your plate – you can always give yourself a smaller serving next time, so less will be wasted.

10 FINGER ON THE PULSE

Make the most of pulses – beans and lentils. They're not just for vegetarians! These underrated foods are full of the soluble fibre that helps lower our cholesterol levels, and are packed with protein, making them a healthy and delicious alternative to meat and animal products, which are higher in fat, particularly the 'bad' saturated fat.

And swap your 'white' foods for 'brown' alternatives. Have wholemeal bread, brown pasta and rice instead of white, and try some of the other tasty grains, such as bulgur, buckwheat, millet and quinoa.

When you eat wholemeal and 'brown' foods, you're getting them in their natural, most nutritious state – when they're processed to make 'white' foods they lose much of their vitamin, mineral and fibre content, and therefore much of their nutritional value.

✓ **If your resolutions wobble then look out for this tick symbol in each chapter, which will give you two pointers to concentrate on.**

FOOD DIARY

How healthy is your diet? The participants in the *You Are What You Eat* television series always get a shock when they see just what they eat in a week! Why not take a notebook and keep a tally of exactly what you eat in a week – you might be surprised, too.

+ Plus points:

How many portions of fruit?
How many portions of vegetables?
How many portions of fish?
How many portions of beans or lentils?
How many portions of wholegrains (wholemeal bread, brown rice or pasta etc.)?

– Minus points:

How many chocolate bars?
How many packets of sweets?
How many ready meals?
How many takeaway meals?
How many cakes or slices of cake?
How many packets of crisps?
How many alcoholic drinks?
How many glasses of fizzy drink?
How many cups of coffee?
How many spoonfuls of sugar in drinks?
How many portions of fried food?

Now you can see where you could make some changes towards a new and healthier you.
   Check again in three months' time to see the progress you've made. If you've followed our lifestyle changes, you'll already be feeling healthier and more positive.

january

A NEW YEAR AND A NEW YOU

Did you enjoy yourself over Christmas and the New Year? Are you perhaps feeling a little guilty about what you ate, and how badly you treated your body over the festive season?

Take another look at the '10 steps to a healthier lifestyle' in the previous chapter – make these your New Year's resolutions and you've laid the foundations for a healthier lifestyle all year round.

NEW YEAR, NEW YOU

Did all those mince pies and savoury nibbles and that enormous Christmas dinner leave you feeling like a beached whale? And what about the boxes of chocolates that simply *had* to be eaten?

And did your exercise programme get brushed aside, because in the whirlwind of Christmas preparations and celebrations, there simply wasn't time?

And don't even *mention* the alcohol!

Chances are, like most of us, you could have been kinder to your body over the last few weeks. And you're probably feeling a bit sluggish and lacklustre, and have perhaps put on a few pounds. But don't feel bad about it – just resolve to start afresh, with a shiny new set of New Year's resolutions.

The New Year is a great time to make a new start – the excesses of Christmas can provide a real motivation for change. You don't need to do everything at once. If you want to jump-start your new lifestyle, pick the resolution where you're the most off-target. Perhaps you never have breakfast, or you're a caffeine fiend. Or if you find that too daunting, ease yourself in gently, with something you won't find so much of a challenge.

Just remember, whatever steps you take, you're making progress.

SAVVY SHOPPING

It's easy to fall into temptation when you're out shopping, and fill your trolley with all those unhealthy foods you might have bought before.

If you do a main weekly shop, try to make a rough meal plan for the week beforehand, so you know what you need to buy. You don't have to plan your family's meals with military precision – you need to have a bit of flexibility in your life. But it's helpful to be able to make a shopping list, so you don't buy things 'just in case we need some of that'.

Try these tips to keep you on the straight and narrow when out shopping:
- Never go shopping when you're hungry or tired – you're more likely to give in to temptation.
- Make a list – and stick to it.
- Only visit the parts of the shops that you have to – you don't *need* to walk down the sweets aisle, do you?
- Consider ordering your shopping online – you're less likely to succumb to impulse buys.
- Look into ordering an organic 'fruit and veggie box' from a local farm or a national company.
- Make the most of special promotions on healthy items – especially store-cupboard foods. But try not to give in to the marketing hype behind processed foods.

Good days, bad days

There are bound to be days when you resort to your old, bad eating habits. Perhaps you had a particularly stressful day, and the temptation of a sweet, sticky treat was just too much to resist.

Don't beat yourself up about it! It's not the end of the world, and tomorrow is a new day. In the words of the old song, just 'pick yourself up, dust yourself down, and start all over again'!

Once you start noticing the wonderful changes in the way you feel, your motivation will increase, and the little 'wobbles' where you fall off the programme will become few and far between.

WEANING FOR GROWN-UPS

Try to wean yourself onto healthier, low-salt, low-sugar, and low-fat tastes. Do it gradually, and you'll hardly notice the difference.

Reducing salt

Most of the salt in our diets comes from the increasing amount of processed food we eat. So the simplest and most effective way to cut down our salt intake is to eat more fresh food. Of course, cutting down on the amount added during cooking and at the table helps, too.

Sweet talking

A little sugar isn't bad for you. It's the kind of sugar, and the amount you eat, that matters. Unfortunately most of us consume too much of the wrong kinds, and when we eat it in preference to other foods, our diets can become less nutritious.

Fat savers

You can cut down the amount of fats in your diet using these tips. But remember, you still need an adequate intake of the 'good' fats found in oily fish, nuts and seeds.

- Make fried food an occasional event, and switch to low-fat cooking methods
- Cut down the amount of butter or spread you put on bread or toast. And, in sandwiches, use low-fat mayonnaise or salad cream instead.
- Read food labels when out shopping, and steer clear of high-fat processed food, particularly when it contains a lot of saturated fat.
- Choose low-fat salad dressings – and it's even healthier to make your own, as manufactured low-fat dressings often contain a lot of artificial ingredients to give them the right consistency. A splash of balsamic vinegar, or vinegar and a little olive oil, on a salad is delicious.

Reading the labels

Become a label sleuth – once you can decipher the food labels, you won't be taken in by any over-hyped marketing claims.

- Some breakfast cereals are alarmingly high in sugar and salt. The best options are no-added sugar/salt muesli and porridge.
- 'No added sugar' doesn't necessarily mean the food is totally virtuous. Although any sweetness may come from natural fruit sugars (which are much better for us than refined sugar), the product may contain artificial sweeteners.
- Foods with 'no artificial preservatives' may still contain natural preservatives such as salt or sugar.
- 'Reduced calorie' simply means it contains fewer calories than the regular version – it may still be high in calories itself.
- Foods labelled 'low fat' *must* contain less than three per cent fat.

Types of sugar – not all sugars are bad

Added sugar is often sucrose, or table sugar, which is quickly used and absorbed by the body, giving a blood-sugar boost that all too quickly fizzles out.

Some fresh foods contain natural sugars. For example, fruit contains fructose, and milk contains lactose. But these sugars are less quickly absorbed by the body, sustaining us for longer. These natural sugars also come packaged with a whole variety of other nutrients, like vitamins, minerals and fibre.

Shop smarter

✔ **For a healthier shopping basket, buy more:**

Fresh fruit and vegetables

Nuts and seeds

Brown rice and wholemeal pasta

Pulses – lentils and beans

Skimmed milk, low-fat fromage frais, and low-fat yogurt

Wholemeal bread and rolls

Skinless chicken and turkey

Oily fish – sardines, pilchards, salmon etc.

✘ **And buy less:**

Meat and meat products

Processed and ready meals

Cream, full-fat milk and full-fat yogurt

Butter and cheese

Chips and crisps

Biscuits and cakes

Sweets and chocolate

What about salt?

Many labels list 'sodium' rather than salt. 1g of sodium is the equivalent of 2.5g of salt. This means that a portion of food with 0.5g of sodium actually contains 1.25g of salt – well on the way to the maximum recommended daily intake of 6g. Salt lurks in a huge variety of processed foods – from tomato ketchup to cornflakes – so it's very easy to go over the limit, even if you don't add salt at the table or in your cooking.

Nutritional information

Ingredients are listed in descending order, with the main ingredient first in the list. Most manufactured foods have a table showing nutrients per portion, and per 100g, and the Food Standards Agency has produced the following guidelines to help us to avoid the 'baddies' in our food.

Ingredient	A LOT per 100g	A LITTLE per 100g
Fat	20g	3g
Saturates (saturated fat)	5g	1g
Sodium	0.5g	0.1g
Salt	1.25g	0.25g
Sugars	10g	2g

You should also try to avoid trans fats, since they have similar (and possibly worse) effects than saturated fats on our cholesterol levels and risk of heart disease.

When all's said and done, the 'best' ingredients lists are the shortest ones, with words you recognise, rather than all those E numbers and unpronounceable chemicals. And wholefoods without ingredients lists – such as fresh vegetables and fruit – are better still!

✔ **THIS MONTH, MAKE SURE YOU:**
- Make it yourself – don't rely on processed meals
- Eat breakfast – a healthy one every day

STORE CUPBOARD STAPLES

There's no need to blitz your store cupboard in order to begin eating a more healthy diet. Just add one new staple to your shopping list each week, and try to buy new items in small quantities so you can see if you like them. When you run out of white rice buy brown rice, when you run out of white pasta replace it with wholemeal pasta. And gradually stock up on flavoursome herbs and spices. Here are some items you could add to the store cupboard:

- **Grains** – rice, quinoa, millet, bulgur wheat, buckwheat, couscous, oats
- **Nuts** – almonds, Brazil nuts, hazelnuts, walnuts, pine nuts, cashew nuts
- **Seeds** – pumpkin seeds, sesame seeds, sunflower seeds
- **Beans** (tinned or dried) – aduki beans, cannellini beans, red kidney beans, chick peas
- **Lentils** – red lentils, continental lentils
- **Flour** – wholewheat plain and self-raising flour, strong bread flour, cornflour, rice flour
- **Tins** – tinned tomatoes, tinned fish (salmon, sardines, mackerel, tuna)
- **Long-life cartons of pure juice** – apple, orange

It's a good idea to have some tins of fruit in juice and no-salt, no-sugar vegetables in your store cupboard. They may not have all the nutrient benefits of fresh, but they're better than nothing if you can't get to the shops in a hurry.

ACTION
GET MOVING

Changing your diet will bring you energy you never believed you had. But food is only part of the story. Now it's time to make the most of it and get moving.

If you thought exercise was all about Day-glo Lycra, scary (and skinny) instructors, high-tech gyms, sweat and exhaustion, think again. Done regularly, even very modest exercise will make a difference to the way you feel.

If you need convincing about the benefits of exercise, the scientific evidence might help convince you.

Exercise:

- Lowers your proportion of body fat, and increases your proportion of body muscle
- Can help weight loss, when combined with a healthy diet
- Lowers your blood pressure
- Lowers your cholesterol level
- Lowers your risk of suffering from heart attacks and strokes
- Lowers your risk of certain types of cancer
- Reduces your risk of diabetes
- Can improve bone density (depending on the type of exercise), therefore reducing your risk of osteoporosis
- Helps you to enjoy a better quality of life, especially as you grow older
- Can improve your mood and state of mind

How much, what type?

Ideally you should exercise for thirty minutes each day, but you can break this down into bite-sized chunks.

If it fits better into your routine, you could aim for twenty minutes to an hour three times a week. Pick a combination of activities so you don't get bored.

Experts recommend that you do some aerobic exercise two to three times a week – you'll learn more about this in May's section on p 83. On other days, do some resistance exercise, or an activity that promotes flexibility, or relaxation.

Different activities complement your day-to-day activities, helping you on the way to overall fitness. Ringing the changes also stops you becoming bored!

Begin gradually and work up to your target. If you start too vigorously, you'll probably hate it, and could injure yourself. But keep at it – it takes time to adopt a new habit.

If you have a chronic health problem (such as obesity, heart problems, diabetes, bone or joint problems), if you're a smoker, or are pregnant, you should check with your doctor before beginning an exercise programme.

Keep motivated

Exercise with a friend – you'll support one another

Join a class or gym – your instructor and classmates will encourage you

Choose an activity you enjoy – some people prefer team sports or classes while others prefer to exercise alone

Exercise ideas

If you like exercising at the gym that's great, and there are often special offers for new members in January. But if you hate the gym, that's fine too. There are plenty of other enjoyable ways to get exercise, and we'll talk about some of them later in this book. But for now how about these:

- Walk instead of driving wherever possible
- Take the stairs rather than the lift
- Join an exercise group that fits into your week
- Get cycling
- Find your nearest ice-skating rink
- Join a dance class
- Try yoga or Pilates
- Buy an exercise video
- When you mow the lawn, or do the housework, put a little extra oomph into it!

Alan Maidens-Taylor

A sober insurance salesman by day, at night 28-year-old Alan Maidens-Taylor transformed himself into a big-drinking drag queen and part-time DJ who would squeeze his enormous twenty-stone and six-foot frame into costumes that then burst at the seams.

Alan was only half that size when he first met his partner, Nathan. He doubled in weight in the eight years since they first met and Nathan wanted the slim old Alan back. So Alan's relationship, as well as his outrageous outfits, were in tatters because of his huge weight gain.

It was clearly time to take action and Nathan was the one who took it. He secretly nominated Alan for *You Are What You Eat*, but when Gillian surprised Alan at his office, Alan took it on his double chin and agreed to go on the regime.

But first he was shocked into facing up to just how bad his eating and drinking habits were. In just one week Alan knocked back a stupendous 110 units of alcohol – that's five times the recommended weekly amount. And that's not all. He missed out on breakfast, a *You Are What You Eat* no-no. And then he would binge on sugary snacks and takeaways.

Alan's scary drinking habits were already wreaking havoc with his body. As well as the enormous weight gain, he had a terrible memory, poor concentration and poor digestion – all associated with drinking too much. And all borne out by the lab tests, which showed Alan was deficient in vitamins B1, B2 and B6, as well as chromium.

You Are What You Eat replaced his nonexistent breakfast with a white bean 'cappuccino' – packed full of B-vitamins, desperately needed nutrients, which the alcohol would have stripped from his system. His liquid lunches were replaced with a cold turkey salad, as turkey contains tryptophan which converts into serotonin, a natural chemical that helps to lift your mood – a much healthier high than the one Alan was seeking out through alcohol.

Then it was eight weeks of healthy eating, lots of exercise and – vitally – no alcohol for Alan.

Alan hit his first wall with breakfast. He claimed eating early made him queasy, and he couldn't face Gillian's quinoa porridge. When she found out that he was feeding it to the dog, Gillian paid a visit and replaced it with a morning smoothie. Much better.

A few weeks later Alan faced another test. On a night out his partner Nathan got really drunk and Alan was sorely tempted to join him. He resisted but felt that Nathan, who did after all nominate him, wasn't being supportive. Gillian took Alan out for a pep talk and Nathan for a telling off.

Six weeks in and, despite being laid up with a damaged wrist and unable to exercise for a week, Alan was making good progress. He felt better and slimmer. At the end of eight weeks, Alan had lost nearly three stone, weighing seventeen stone and three pounds, and had lost nearly nine inches around his waist.

MENU PLANNER
JANUARY IDEAS

 **JANUARY BEST BUYS**

Make the most of:

Brussels sprouts

Carrots

Parsnips

Celeriac

Swedes

Turnips

Pears

Menu 1

Breakfast — Spicy scrambled egg on a wholemeal bagel

Lunch — Chunky winter vegetable soup

Dinner — Quick bean chilli

Mincemeat and orange tartlets

Menu 2

Breakfast — Wholemeal muffins with spicy tomato and mushrooms

Lunch — Zesty herb-and-nut stuffed trout

Dinner — Speedy spaghetti bolognese

Hot rice pudding with berry fruits

Menu 1
☼ Spicy scrambled egg on a bagel

4 eggs

¼ teaspoon ready-prepared chilli or to taste

1 skinned, finely chopped tomato

½ finely chopped green pepper

2tbsp skimmed milk (optional)

4 wholemeal bagels (or wholemeal English muffins)

Salt and pepper

Serves 4

1. Add ¼ tsp sunflower oil to a saucepan and gently fry the pepper, tomato and chilli until just softened. Remove from the heat.
2. Beat the eggs in a bowl. Add milk if liked. Season with a little salt and pepper.
3. Pour the beaten eggs into the saucepan and place over a medium heat. Continue stirring until the eggs are lightly scrambled.
4. Spoon onto toasted wholemeal bagels (or muffins) and serve with grilled tomatoes or mushrooms.

☀ Chunky winter vegetable soup

1tbsp sunflower oil

1 onion, chopped

1 large leek, trimmed, thinly sliced, rinsed and shaken dry

1 large garlic clove, crushed

1 large carrot, about 250g, diced

1 large turnip, about 250g, cored and diced

1 piece butternut squash (350g peeled weight), seeds and fibres removed and diced

1 bay leaf and several sprigs of fresh parsley and thyme, tied together

600ml ready-made vegetable stock

1 can (400g) chopped tomatoes

Pinch of caster sugar

Salt and pepper

Chopped fresh parsley, to garnish

Wholemeal rolls, to serve

Serves 4

1. Heat the oil in a large saucepan or flameproof casserole over a medium heat. Add the onion and leek and stir for 3 minutes. Stir in the garlic and continue stirring for a further 2–3 minutes until the onion is soft, but not brown.
2. Add the carrot, turnip and squash to the pan and stir around for 5 minutes or until they are just starting to soften.
3. Add the herbs, then stir in the stock, tomatoes with their juices, sugar and salt and pepper to taste. Slowly bring to the boil, then reduce the heat, cover the pan and leave the soup to simmer for 30 minutes until the vegetables are tender.
4. Remove the herbs and adjust the seasoning. Ladle into bowls, sprinkle with parsley and serve with wholemeal rolls.

> **Health Fact:** Garlic contains a sulphur-based compound called allicin, which helps lower cholesterol levels, reducing our risk of heart disease.

☽ Quick bean chilli

1. Heat the oil in a large saucepan or casserole and gently cook the onion, celery and garlic for about 5 minutes until the onion has softened, stirring occasionally. Add the chilli powder and cook for 30 seconds, stirring constantly.

2. Next add the peppers and courgettes and cook with the other vegetables for 3–4 minutes, stirring regularly. Tip the tomatoes into the pan, then half-fill the can with cold water and pour over the vegetables. Add the tomato purée and bouillon powder or stock cube.

3. Bring to the boil, then reduce the heat and simmer gently for 15 minutes, stirring occasionally. Add the beans to the pan and continue cooking for a further 5 minutes until all the vegetables are tender, the beans are hot and the sauce has thickened. Stir regularly.

4. Serve with freshly cooked brown rice, topped with spoonfuls of fat-free bio-yogurt.

Health fact: Peppers are rich in vitamin C, which supports the immune system, and betacarotene, an antioxidant which the body uses to help protect against heart disease and cancer.

1tbsp virgin olive oil

1 large mild onion, peeled and chopped

2 celery sticks, trimmed and sliced

1 garlic clove, peeled and crushed

½–1tsp hot chilli powder (to taste)

1 red and 1 yellow or orange pepper, deseeded and cut into 2.5cm chunks

2 small courgettes, trimmed and cut into 1cm slices

1 can (400g) chopped tomatoes

2tbsp tomato purée

2tsp organic vegetable bouillon (stock) powder or 1 organic vegetable stock cube

1 can (410g) 'no-salt' red kidney beans, drained and rinsed

Freshly cooked wholegrain (brown) rice and fat-free bio-yogurt

Serves 4

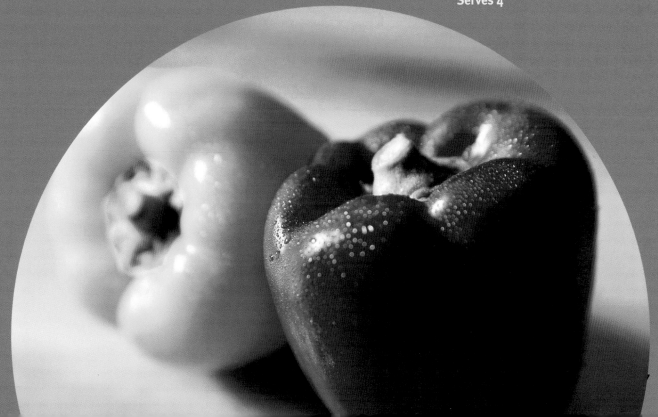

Mincemeat and orange tartlets

100g sultanas

100g raisins

6 fresh dates, stoned and chopped

1 apple, peeled, quartered, cored and coarsely grated

1tsp ground mixed spice

Freshly squeezed juice and finely grated zest of 1 medium orange

6–8 sheets filo pastry (thawed if frozen)

2tsp sunflower oil

25g dried cranberries (optional)

15g flaked almonds

Makes 24

1 Mix the sultanas, raisins, dates, apples, mixed spice, orange juice and zest together in a large bowl, then set aside for 1–2 hours to allow the flavours to infuse and the fruit to swell.

2 Preheat the oven to 200°C/Gas 6. Taking one sheet of pastry at a time, cut into three or four long strips – each about 6cm wide – depending on the size of the pastry. (Keep remaining pastry covered so it doesn't dry out.)

3 Brush very lightly with oil and gently fold and scrunch each strip into a nest shape to line the holes of a twelve-cup Yorkshire pudding tin. Add 2 heaped teaspoons of the dried fruit filling to each pastry case.

4 Top with a couple of cranberries and add a few flaked almonds. Bake for about 12 minutes until the pastry is crisp and golden. Cool for 2–3 minutes, then carefully remove from the tin. Repeat with remaining pastry and filling. Serve warm or cold.

Dates provide calcium, iron, fibre and betacarotene. They contribute an intense sweetness to the recipe, but the fibre helps slow down the natural sugars' uptake into the bloodstream.

Some dried fruits are sweetened and glazed, so look carefully at the list of ingredients and try to go for more natural organic versions.

Menu 2

☼ Wholemeal muffins with spicy tomato and mushrooms

1 Roughly chop the tomatoes and slice the mushrooms.
2 Place the chopped tomato in a saucepan with the Worcestershire sauce, tomato purée and water.
3 Cook over a low heat until the tomatoes are soft. Add the mushrooms and cook for a further 3 minutes.
4 Cut each muffin in half and toast. Spoon the hot tomato-and-mushroom mixture over the muffins and serve immediately.

> **Health fact:** Most vegetables lose vitamins when cooked, but tomatoes are an exception – cooking them actually increases their nutritional benefit.

4 wholemeal muffins

200g mushrooms, washed and sliced

4 tomatoes, roughly chopped

2tsp Worcestershire sauce

1tbsp tomato purée

2tbsp water

Serves 4

☼ Zesty herb-and-nut stuffed trout

1 Remove any tiny bones from the fillets using tweezers, if necessary.
2 Lightly oil an electric health grill and preheat – you can also use a ridged griddle.
3 Mix the stuffing ingredients in a small bowl.
4 Place two of the trout fillets skin-side down on a board and spoon the stuffing on top. Cover with remaining fillets to sandwich the filling and lift carefully onto the grill or griddle.
5 If using the electric health grill, close the lid and grill for about 5 minutes until cooked through. If using a griddle cook for 3 minutes on each side or until cooked.
6 Serve with lots of freshly cooked seasonal vegetables or a large salad and lemon wedges for squeezing.

> **Health fact:** Trout is an excellent source of the essential omega-3 fatty acids, which help lower the 'bad' kind of cholesterol and promote healthy skin.

8 x 115g fresh trout fillets

Freshly ground black pepper

Sunflower oil, for greasing

For the stuffing:

30g flaked almonds

30g fresh wholemeal breadcrumbs

4 spring onions, trimmed and finely sliced

6tbsp roughly chopped curly parsley

Finely grated zest of 1 lemon

Serves 4

☾ Speedy spaghetti bolognese

1tbsp olive oil

500g turkey mince, preferably free-range or organic

1 onion, peeled and chopped

1 plump garlic clove, peeled and crushed

2 carrots, peeled and cut into 1cm dice

1 courgette, trimmed and cut into 1cm dice

1 red pepper, deseeded and cut into 1cm dice

2 x 400g cans chopped tomatoes

1tsp mixed freeze-dried herbs

Half an organic vegetable stock cube

2tsp cornflour mixed with 1tbsp cold water

Wholewheat spaghetti and fresh basil leaves, to serve

Serves 6 (4 to serve and 2 to freeze)

1 Heat the oil in a large saucepan or flameproof casserole over a gentle heat. Add the turkey and cook for 3 minutes, stirring to break up the meat. Stir in the onion and garlic and cook for 2 minutes.

2 Add the carrots, courgette and pepper and cook with the mince for 5 minutes, stirring regularly, until all the vegetables are beginning to soften.

3 Tip the tomatoes into the pan, sprinkle with herbs and add the stock cube. Bring to the boil, then reduce the heat and simmer for 15 minutes, stirring occasionally until the vegetables are just cooked and the turkey is tender.

4 Stir in the cornflour mixture and cook for a few seconds until the sauce is thickened. Serve with freshly cooked wholewheat spaghetti, garnished with basil leaves and a large fresh, crunchy salad.

TIP

● This Bolognese can be served in a variety of ways: spooned into baked potatoes or tossed with gluten-free pasta; enjoyed just as it is with seasonal vegetables; or used as a stuffing for baked squash or marrow.

Hot rice pudding with berry fruits

50g pudding rice

600ml skimmed milk

1tbsp caster sugar or 1tsp runny honey

2 strips of lemon rind

Grated nutmeg (optional)

Low-fat spread to grease dish

Fresh or tinned berry fruits, to serve

Serves 4

1 Preheat the oven to 150°C/Gas 2.

2 Wash the rice and drain well. Grease a 750ml ovenproof dish with a little low-fat spread, add the rice and stir in the milk. Leave the rice to soak in the milk for 30 minutes.

3 Add the lemon rind and sprinkle over the sugar or honey. Grate nutmeg over, if liked.

4 Place in the oven and bake for 2–2½ hours. Stir the pudding after the first 45 minutes.

5 Spoon the rice pudding into 4 bowls. Serve the rice pudding topped with tinned or fresh berry fruits.

Health fact: Skimmed milk contains virtually the same amount of calcium as semi-skimmed or full-fat milk – but much less fat.

Turkey is a good source of lean protein. It provides good amounts of the B-vitamins and useful amounts of iron and zinc.

february

FOODS TO FIGHT FATIGUE

How do you feel today? Just OK? If the best you ever achieve is 'OK', your diet could be holding you back. If you're not well nourished, your body won't function at its best, and you'll also be less able to fight off bugs and germs.

- Get fresh – eating plenty of fresh food
- Eat 5-a-day – at least five portions of fruit and vegetables

MICRONUTRIENTS – MACRO-BENEFITS

Good nutrition isn't just about protein, fats and carbohydrates – you also need enough vitamins and minerals. Although these so-called micronutrients are only needed in tiny quantities, they're vital to keep our body processes running smoothly.

Unfortunately, a lot of us don't get enough vitamins and minerals – especially vitamins A and C, folic acid and iron. We may also be lacking in other micronutrients, such as the B-vitamins, if we're under stress, or rely a lot on processed foods. Certain groups of people also have increased demands for particular nutrients – for example, women need extra calcium to build and maintain healthy bones and prevent the bone-thinning disease osteoporosis, and pregnancy brings a whole range of increased nutritional demands. Vegans may not get enough vitamin B12 or vitamin D in their diet. Vitamin D deficiency can also be a problem for people with dark skin, or people who don't go outside much in sunlight, since a major source of this vitamin is from the effect of sunlight on the skin.

MICRO-NUTRIENTS

VITAMIN	ROLE	SOURCES
Vitamin A	Maintains healthy eyes and skin, supports the immune system	Liver, oily fish, eggs, spinach, broccoli, plus yellow and orange foods, such as carrots, sweet potato, apricots, cantaloupe
B Vitamins (Vitamins B1, B2, B3, B6, B12)	Formation of healthy blood cells, maintenance of a healthy nervous system, release of energy from food	Wholegrains, meat, fish, eggs, pulses, nuts, seeds and vegetables
Vitamin C	Supports the immune system, promotes healing, helps absorption of iron from the diet	Fruit (especially kiwi fruit, blackcurrants, strawberries, citrus fruits), peppers, potatoes
Vitamin D	Helps the body absorb and use calcium, so needed for healthy bones and teeth	Oily fish, meat, eggs, dairy products, plus sunlight on the skin
Vitamin E	Helps maintain healthy blood vessels, supports the immune system, protects the body's cells from harmful substances	Wheat germ, nuts and seeds and their oils, wholemeal bread, avocado
Folic acid	Absorption of nutrients, prevention of anaemia. May also reduce the risk of heart disease. Folic acid is particularly important for pregnant women	Green leafy vegetables, beans and lentils, brown rice, wheat germ, eggs

MINERAL	ROLE	SOURCES
Iron	Needed for healthy red blood cells and prevention of anaemia	Red meat, beans and lentils, green vegetables, dried fruit
Calcium	Helps build and maintain healthy bones and teeth	Dairy foods, fish where the bones are eaten (e.g. tinned sardines and salmon), tofu, green leafy vegetables
Zinc	Supports the immune system, healthy skin	Meat, fish, chicken, eggs, dairy products, green leafy vegetables, beans and lentils

FATIGUE

It's a sad reflection on our modern lifestyles, that so many of us feel tired all the time. As with so many other aspects of our wellbeing, diet can play an important role in whether we feel bright-eyed and bushy-tailed, or so weary we're hardly able to haul ourselves out of bed in the morning.

First of all, you need to ensure that your tiredness isn't caused by something that's nothing to do with your diet, which could mean a visit to your doctor for a checkup.

Some non-dietary causes of tiredness include:
- Lack of sleep (see Action, p 39)
- Stress (see p 50)
- An underactive thyroid gland
- Diabetes
- Depression

Don't panic!

There's no need to get obsessed with individual vitamins. The foods that are rich in those vital vitamins and minerals are exactly the same nutritious foods that make up your new, healthy eating plan – low-fat protein sources, complex carbohydrates and plenty of fruit and vegetables. Eat healthy foods, and the vitamins and minerals will fall into place.

Why iron?

Iron is needed to make haemoglobin, a pigment found in red blood cells that transports oxygen around the body, releasing it where it's needed.

Oxygen is needed to 'fuel' the body, so if the oxygen doesn't get to where it should be, your body's cells will feel 'starved', and you'll feel tired and run down.

Iron friends and foes

Some foods help your absorption of iron, while others hinder it.

◆ Vitamin C eaten at the same time as iron-containing foods really boosts your iron uptake, so drink a glass of orange juice with your meal.

◆ High-fibre diets, especially insoluble fibre such as bran, hinders iron absorption. But fibre is good for you, and vegetarian iron sources are high in fibre themselves. To maximise your iron absorption, just don't add extra fibre to your meals, for example by sprinkling wheat bran on them.

◆ Tea and coffee contain tannins, which interfere with iron uptake. Don't drink them with meals, and save them for occasional between-meal treats.

◆ Spinach and rhubarb contain plant chemicals called oxalates, which also hinder iron absorption. Don't serve them with iron-rich foods.

THE IMPORTANCE OF IRON

The main diet-related cause of fatigue is iron-deficiency anaemia, and your doctor can arrange a blood test for this. Eight per cent of women and two per cent of men are anaemic, and if this is the case for you, your doctor may prescribe iron supplements. However, a lot more people have low iron stores – not enough to make them anaemic, but enough to cause them to feel below par. If this is the case for you, ask your doctor if you should take an iron supplement – don't be tempted to take them without advice, as too much iron isn't good for you either. Your doctor may say that you don't need supplements, but simply need to increase the amount of iron-rich foods in your diet.

Some people are more at risk from anaemia and low iron stores. Women lose iron every month when they have their periods. Children, and especially teenagers, need extra iron because of the muscle they are gaining, and pregnant women need more to build their babies' muscle and red blood cells.

If your iron levels need boosting, try to increase your intake of iron-rich foods. Iron from animal sources is easiest for your body to absorb and use – you'll find it in liver (though you should avoid liver if you're pregnant), red meat and eggs. Iron from vegetarian sources, such as beans, spinach and other green leafy vegetables, and apricots, is less available to your body, so vegetarians need to make sure they maximise their absorption of this vital mineral. One way is to eat vitamin C-rich foods or drink a glass of orange juice with your meal as these will help iron absorption.

Stress can also make you feel tired and frazzled. You'll find more on dealing with stress in the next section of this book.

ACTION
A GOOD NIGHT'S SLEEP

Not getting enough sleep makes us feel tired and fuzzy-headed. It can affect our memory and ability to think clearly, and make us more likely to have accidents.

While a single disturbed night may simply make us cranky and irritable the next day, chronic, sustained insomnia can seriously affect our quality of life.

So how much sleep do we need? There are no hard-and-fast rules about how much sleep is adequate, but most adults need around eight hours' sleep per night. Children generally need more, and the elderly tend to require less sleep.

Sleep enemies

- Alcohol – it may help you drop off to sleep, but it can disturb your sleep later in the night.
- Stimulants such as tobacco and caffeine. You may think a cigarette before bed makes you feel relaxed, but nicotine is actually a stimulant. Don't drink coffee in the evening, and if you're particularly sensitive to caffeine, avoid coffee after lunchtime.
- Watching TV, eating, reading exciting books or discussing emotional issues in bed.
- Heavy meals less than three hours before bedtime.
- Vigorous exercise in the evening, and daytime naps (though these are not a problem for everyone).

Tips to help you sleep

- Ensure your bedroom is relaxing and tranquil.
- Minimise noise and light extremes with earplugs and window blinds.
- Keep your bedroom at a comfortable temperature – neither too hot nor too cold.
- A light snack at bedtime can aid sleep. Milk contains sleep-promoting tryptophan, and oatcakes or a low-sugar biscuit help stabilise blood-sugar levels.
- If you have to get up during the night, switch on a night light or a dimmer switch rather than the main light, as bright light will jolt you wide awake, making it harder to get back to sleep.

MENU PLANNER
FEBRUARY IDEAS

 **FEBRUARY BEST BUYS**

Make the most of:

Brussels sprouts

Carrots

Parsnips

Swedes

Turnips

Menu 1

 **Breakfast** — Banana and cinnamon porridge

Lunch — Spinach and ricotta pancakes

Dinner — Moroccan-style chicken and chickpea stew

Baked pears with ginger and almonds

Menu 2

Breakfast — Spicy egg, pepper and tomato pan breakfast

 Lunch — Quick mushroom soup

 Dinner — Roasted cod with leek mash and vine tomatoes

Orange and almond sponge

Menu 1
☀ Banana and cinnamon porridge

1. Place the oats, milk and water in a medium, nonstick saucepan. Peel and slice the banana into the pan and stir in the sultanas and cinnamon.
2. Bring to the boil over a medium heat, stirring constantly. Reduce the heat and simmer gently for about 5 minutes, stirring regularly until the oats are tender.
3. Spoon into four warmed bowls and decorate with a pinch of ground cinnamon if liked.

100g porridge oats

300ml skimmed milk

450ml cold water

1 large banana

75g sultanas

¼ tsp ground cinnamon, plus extra to decorate

Serves 4

☼ Spinach and ricotta pancakes

1. Place the eggs, flour and skimmed milk in a bowl or food processor, and whisk or process until the mixture is smooth. Transfer the batter to a jug.
2. Heat a large nonstick frying pan on the hob and drizzle with a little of the oil. Wipe around the base of the pan carefully with a thick wad of folded kitchen paper to lightly grease.
3. Add a little of the batter and tilt the pan so the base is evenly coated. Cook for about 3 minutes until set, then loosen the edges with a round-bladed knife and flip over. Cook the other side for around 2 minutes until golden. Transfer to a plate and continue making pancakes until all the batter is used
4. Preheat the oven to 200°C/Gas 6. Heat the oil for the filling in a large saucepan and gently fry the onion and garlic until softened. Add the spinach leaves and nutmeg. Cook for 4–5 minutes until wilted, stirring regularly. Stand for 5 minutes.
5. Tip the onion, garlic, spinach and ricotta into a food processor and blend until well combined. If you do not have a food processor you can combine the filling mixture in a bowl. Spoon roughly a sixth of the cheese mixture down the side of one of the pancakes and roll up.
6. Place in a lightly oiled, ovenproof dish. Fill and roll the remaining pancakes until all the mixture is used. Pour the pasta sauce over the pancakes, sprinkle with Parmesan and bake for 25–30 minutes until hot throughout.

For the batter:

2 medium eggs

100g wholemeal flour

250ml skimmed milk

Olive oil, for greasing

For the filling:

1tsp olive oil

1 small onion, peeled and chopped

1 garlic clove, peeled and crushed

75g baby spinach leaves, washed and drained

1 pot (250g) ricotta cheese

¼ tsp ground nutmeg

Freshly ground black pepper

For the topping:

1 jar (325g) low-fat tomato pasta sauce

10g Parmesan cheese, finely grated

Serves 4

☽ Moroccan-style chicken and chickpea stew

1tbsp virgin olive oil

2 garlic cloves, peeled and crushed

2 medium onions, peeled and sliced

2 boneless chicken breasts, preferably free range or organic, skinned and cut into bite-sized pieces

1 small bunch fresh coriander (about 10g), roughly chopped

About 10g fresh mint, roughly chopped

1tsp hot chilli powder

1tsp ground cumin

½ tsp ground cinnamon

1 can (400g) chopped tomatoes

1 can (410g) 'no-salt' chickpeas, drained and rinsed

75g 'no-soak' dried apricots, chopped

25g blanched almonds

Half an organic vegetable stock cube

Serves 4

1. Put the oil, garlic, onions, chicken, herbs and spices in a large saucepan or flameproof casserole and toss well together. Place over a medium heat and cook for 5 minutes, stirring regularly.
2. Add all the remaining ingredients, then refill the empty tomato can with cold water and pour into the pan. Bring to the boil, then reduce the heat and simmer gently for 25–30 minutes until the chicken is tender, stirring occasionally.
3. Serve with a crunchy salad or lots of steamed or lightly boiled green vegetables and couscous tossed with sliced spring onions and a few sultanas, if liked.

TIPS

- Couscous is made from wheat, so may not be suitable for people on gluten-free diets. You could try using cooked quinoa, brown rice or millet instead.
- To make a vegetarian version of this dish, simply leave out the chicken and add a can of drained and rinsed red kidney beans to the pot.

Baked pears with ginger and almonds

4 dessert pears, halved and cored

2 preserved stem ginger balls (about 35g), drained and cut into small dice

15g flaked almonds

1tbsp stem ginger syrup

100ml cold water

Virtually fat-free fromage frais or fat-free bio-yogurt, to serve

Serves 4

1. Preheat the oven to 200°C/Gas 6. Place the pears in a shallow ovenproof dish, cut side up. Sprinkle with the stem ginger and then the almonds. Spoon the syrup over the top.
2. Pour the water into the base of the dish and cover with foil. Bake for 20 minutes, then take out of the oven and discard the foil. Carefully spoon the syrupy juices over the pears. Return to the oven, uncovered, for a further 15 minutes or until the pears are tender and lightly browned.
3. Serve with fromage frais or bio-yogurt.

Health fact: Pears contain useful amounts of vitamin C, potassium and fibre.

Chickpeas are an excellent source of protein and soluble fibre and they also contain a useful amount of iron, needed for healthy red blood cells and preventing anaemia.

Menu 2

☀ Spicy egg, pepper and tomato pan breakfast

1 Quarter the peppers, deseed, and cook under a hot grill until the skins begin to blister. Set aside for 10 minutes, covered with a clean tea towel, then remove the skins and thinly slice the peppers.
2 Place the tomatoes, garlic (if used), sugar and water into a nonstick frying pan. Season with pepper. Bring to the boil and gently simmer for 2 minutes. Add the pepper strips and cook for 2 minutes more.
3 Make 4 wells in the mixture and break an egg into each. Cook gently until the eggs are just set. Sprinkle over a little paprika or Cajun spice, if liked. Serve immediately with triangles of crisp toast.

> **Health fact:** The tomatoes and peppers make this a breakfast packed with antioxidants that help protect the body from free radicals – oxygen molecules that can damage the body's cells.

1 can (400g) of chopped tomatoes

2 red or yellow peppers

1 clove garlic (optional)

4 medium eggs

Pinch of paprika or Cajun spice (optional)

75ml of water

1tsp olive oil

½ tsp brown sugar

Freshly ground black pepper

Serves 4

☀ Quick mushroom soup

1 Wash the mushrooms well. Slice all the mushrooms and the onion.
2 Heat the oil in a large saucepan and gently cook the mushrooms, onion and garlic for about 5 minutes until they are softened.
3 Add 600ml cold water and the vegetable bouillon powder. Bring to the boil, then reduce the heat and simmer for 8 minutes. Remove from the heat and cool for at least 10 minutes.
4 Remove roughly a third of the mushrooms and onions with a slotted spoon and set aside. Carefully blend the remaining soup, in batches if necessary, using a stick blender, liquidiser or food processor.
5 Return to the pan and stir in the reserved mushrooms and onions. Add the milk and parsley and heat through gently before serving. Season to taste with ground black pepper.

> **Health fact:** Shiitake mushrooms contain natural plant chemicals (phyto-chemicals) that are believed to help strengthen the immune system.

450g assorted mushrooms, such as chestnut, portabellini and shiitake

1 medium onion, peeled and quartered

1tbsp olive oil

2 garlic cloves, peeled and crushed

2tsp organic vegetable bouillon (stock) powder

150ml skimmed milk

2tbsp chopped fresh parsley

Freshly ground black pepper

Serves 4

☽ Roasted cod with leek mash and vine tomatoes

650g potatoes, preferably Maris Piper

1tbsp virgin olive oil, plus extra for greasing

2 medium leeks, trimmed and thinly sliced

1 garlic clove, peeled and crushed

2tbsp virtually fat-free fromage frais

4 skinless cod or other firm white-fish fillets (each about 150g)

4 strings of vine tomatoes, each holding around 6 small tomatoes

1tbsp fresh thyme leaves (from 2–3 sprigs), preferably lemon thyme

Freshly ground black pepper

Serves 4

1 Preheat the oven to 200°C/Gas 6. Half-fill a large saucepan with cold water and bring to the boil. Peel the potatoes and cut into rough 4cm chunks.

2 Carefully add the potatoes to the water and return to the boil. Cook for about 20 minutes until very tender. Heat 2tsp of the oil in a large frying pan and cook the leeks and garlic for 10–12 minutes until softened, stirring occasionally.

3 Place the cod on a lightly oiled baking tray and sprinkle with the thyme and ground black pepper. Bake for 12–15 minutes until cooked through – depending on thickness. Carefully add the tomatoes to the tray with the cod after it has been cooking for 5 minutes.

4 Drain the potatoes in a colander then return to the pan. Add the fromage frais and mash using a potato masher until smooth. Add the cooked leeks and warm through over a medium heat until hot, stirring regularly. Season to taste with ground black pepper.

5 Spoon potato and leeks onto 4 warmed plates and top with a piece of roasted cod and a string of tomatoes. Serve just as it is or add a few freshly cooked fine green beans.

Cod is a great source of protein and extremely low in fat. Other white fish such as haddock also work well, or you could choose a more sustainable white fish such as hoki.

Orange and almond sponge

1 Lightly oil a 1.2-litre oval pie dish and line the base neatly with baking parchment. Place in the top of a steamer with water underneath.

2 Separate the eggs and place the yolks in one medium bowl and the whites in another. Beat the egg yolks and the sugar together using an electric whisk, until light and fluffy. Stir in the almonds, baking powder, sultanas, orange zest and juice.

3 Whisk the egg whites until stiff using a clean electric whisk.

4 Take one tablespoon of the egg white and fold it into the almond mixture to loosen. Gently fold in the remaining egg white using a large metal spoon.

5 Spoon the batter into the prepared dish and cover loosely with lightly oiled foil. Put the lid on the pan and steam for about 30 minutes until the cake is risen and cooked through.

6 Carefully remove the dish from the steamer using an oven cloth and cut the cake into wedges. Sprinkle with icing sugar. Serve with tinned or fresh berries and fat-free bio-yoghurt, fromage frais or single cream, and a drizzle of honey if liked.

Sunflower oil for greasing

2 medium free-range eggs

50g light-brown muscovado sugar

1 pack (100g) ground almonds

1tsp baking powder

100g sultanas

Finely grated zest and juice of 1 medium orange

150g fresh raspberries (optional)

1tsp golden icing sugar, to decorate (optional)

Fat-free bio-yogurt, fromage frais or single cream and clear honey, to serve

Serves 4–6

Health fact: Eggs are a source of vitamin D, which is essential for healthy bone formation, and also provide good amounts of vitamins A, E, B2 and B12.

march

CALMING FOODS FOR STRESS-BUSTING

Stress is impossible to escape in the modern world. A small amount of pressure is actually good for us, but constant stress can be very damaging to our health.

QUICK QUIZ
Are you stressed?

1 Are there not enough hours in the day to do all you need to do?

2 Do you take on too many commitments?

3 Are you reluctant to ask for help?

4 Do you attempt too many tasks at once?

5 Do you try to carry everyone else's problems and responsibilities?

6 Do you have no time to call your own?

If you answered 'yes' to three or more of these questions, it's time for action. Stress saps our energy so it pays to take some positive steps.

UNDER PRESSURE

In an emergency, the stress reaction sends a rush of adrenalin coursing through our system, giving us super-quick reactions and a boost of physical strength. Athletes say that the tension that builds up before a race helps them to perform at their best.

But it's the kind of chronic, long-term stress so many of us are under that can play havoc with our health – our bodies set the same stress reaction in motion, but there's no outlet for all those hormones and all that energy. Chronic stress can raise our blood pressure, decrease the effectiveness of our immune systems (so that we're more vulnerable to every bug and germ that comes along) and generally spoil our quality of life.

The body can't tell the difference between a life-or-death emergency and the stresses that assail us every day, from traffic jams and call centres, to supermarket queues and computer glitches. Whether the situation is serious or trivial, the stress reaction springs into action, and because the body believes this could be a matter of life or death, this reaction takes precedence over normal body processes like digestion and repair.

Goodbye, good intentions

Stress all too easily sends our healthy eating intentions out of the window. Eating healthily can seem so much less important when it's hard enough to get through the day without crumbling. Some people overeat when under stress, especially junk food, with the expected effects on their weight and health. Others find it hard to eat, which can make them feel even worse as they become tired and headachy, and their resistance to minor illnesses is compromised.

Whether it's overindulging on junk food or undereating, they both mean our bodies are starved of nutrients – and at stressful times when our bodies really need nutritional nurturing. This kind of eating pattern also sets our blood-sugar levels roller-coasting, playing havoc with our energy levels and state of mind.

Maintaining the body on a constant state of alert, ready for anything, is nutritionally very demanding – it's hardly surprising we begin to feel run down! As our bodies pump out the adrenalin and other stress hormones that give us that sudden rush of panic, or that constant feeling of tension, we use up more nutrients than when we're coasting through life on an even keel. And as the nutrient levels run down, our bodies find it harder and harder to cope with stress – it's a downward spiral.

Stress can also upset our digestion. Many people suffer from upset stomachs before an important event, or when they're under chronic stress. And if our digestive system isn't functioning at its best, we won't be digesting and absorbing our food properly – even if we are eating healthily, we may not be gaining the full benefits from all those nutrients.

If we're well nourished, and then a stressful time hits us, our bodies are better able to cope. But if we haven't been eating healthily beforehand, stressful times can quickly send us spiralling into a malnourished state.

So, how to deal with stress? A multi-pronged attack is best.

- Begin from a firm foundation – it's best if you're well nourished.
- Tackle the stress in your life – try our 'stress busters' (see page 52).
- Eat regularly and don't skip meals – it's especially important that you don't get hungry and jittery when you're under stress. Keep your blood-sugar levels nice and even, and you'll be less likely to reach for an unhealthy 'prop' to get you through that tricky situation.
- Concentrate on 'slow fuel' food – once again, this will help maintain your blood-sugar levels on an even keel.
- Top up your nutrients – fill up with foods rich in the nutrients your body needs in stressful times.

NUTRIENTS FOR STRESSFUL TIMES

In times of stress, the body has an increased need for particular nutrients, as these are the ones that are depleted fastest when we're under pressure. When you're stressed, pay particular attention to your intake of:

- Low-fat protein – most of us eat more than enough protein, so quantity is rarely a problem. Concentrate on quality – choose healthy sources such as chicken, turkey, fish and pulses such as beans and lentils.
- Complex carbohydrates (starchy foods) – a stressed body needs more fuel. Fill up with wholemeal bread and brown pasta, brown rice and wholegrains such as bulgur, buckwheat and millet.
- Vitamin C – when we're stressed, our bodies use up vitamin C especially quickly. Top it up with citrus fruits, kiwi fruits, strawberries, blackberries, peppers, and lightly cooked vegetables.
- B-vitamins – from wholegrains, meat, poultry, nuts and bananas.

All of the following can be symptoms of stress:

Anxiety	Dry mouth
Clammy hands	Feeling 'wound up'
Racing heart	Panic attacks
Migraines	Depression
Upset stomach	Tiredness
Insomnia	

If stress is seriously affecting your life, ask your doctor for advice.

Danger points

When we're stressed, we may have trouble sleeping, and become anxious or depressed. We may turn to alcohol, or stimulants such as coffee and cigarettes, in order to cope. Sadly, these props that we lean on in desperation send our poor bodies even further out of balance.

The caffeine crutch

Caffeine and stress are not a good mix. Caffeine can disrupt your sleep patterns, raise stress hormones and make you feel jittery and anxious. It will actually make you feel more stressed.

So cut down on caffeine. Switch to decaffeinated coffee and tea, or caffeine-free alternatives such as 'grain' coffee substitutes, Rooibos tea, and herbal or fruit teas.

Quick-fix stress busters

Are there times when you can feel your anxiety rising? Sometimes all that is needed to put the brakes on is a quick switch to doing something else. Try these tactics – you might be surprised how well they work.

- Make yourself a cup of herbal tea, and drink it slowly, savouring every mouthful of the flavour
- Slip off your shoes, wiggle your toes and rotate your feet – a great trick in the office, when no one can see your wiggling feet
- Close your eyes and take a few moments to visualise the places that invoke special memories for you
- Sit quietly and write down five things that have made you feel happy in the last week
- Take five deep breaths and then stand and do a few gentle stretching exercises

✔ THIS MONTH, MAKE SURE YOU:

- Cut down on caffeine – if you're feeling stressed, try to resist the temptation to use it as a crutch
- Cut down on sugar and salt

STRESS BUSTERS

Lighten up your lifestyle

- Learn to prioritise your tasks and concentrate on them one at a time. Don't even try to be a superman or superwoman – encourage other members of the household to share the load.
- Be realistic and learn to politely say 'no' when someone asks you to take on one commitment too many.
- Learn to see when a problem is someone else's, not yours.
- Don't be too proud to ask for help or take it when it is offered.
- Make a list of the stresses in your life and work out positive ways to reduce those that you can. And don't worry about the rest!
- De-clutter your home and workplace – mess makes you feel more stressed.
- Plan breaks into your day – try to have twenty minutes during your morning and afternoon routine that's exclusively 'me time'.
- Try to cut down on alcohol and cigarettes – relying on them as a crutch is a slippery slope.
- You deserve regular treats – have a manicure or a haircut, or go bowling, to the movies or the theatre.
- Make plans, so that you always have something special to look forward to – it could be a day out, a weekend away or a longer break.
- Take up relaxation or meditation.
- Have a relaxing massage. Aromatherapy massages are especially soothing.

FREE UP SOME 'ME TIME'

Do you spend your evenings on autopilot? Rush home from work, put the washing machine on, run round with the vacuum cleaner, supervise homework, prepare the evening meal, wash up, catch up on household paperwork then crash out exhausted in front of the television until bedtime?

If so, try to slot in just fifteen minutes of wind-down time as soon as you come home. It's a simple way to shake off the tensions of the day and let you start the evening feeling more positive and with renewed energy. You could take a shower and change into something comfortable for the evening, go for a short walk, potter in the garden, or just read the newspaper with a cup of tea.

RESCUE YOUR WEEKEND

Is your weekend like a frantic game of catch-up – catching up with the housework, washing, ironing, cooking, cleaning the car, returning the library books? How often do you say, 'I'll do that at the weekend.' There are still only 24 hours in the day . . . so be realistic and don't try to do too much. Weekends should be a time for relaxing, spending time with the family, getting out into the fresh air, and recharging your batteries.

Try to find ways to spread the workload. Get the rest of the family involved in weekend chores – and on other days of the week. Work out how many regular tasks you fit into a weekend and see if any could be moved to another day of the week – after all, the car doesn't have to be washed on a Saturday, or the windows cleaned on a Sunday.

Eating out doesn't have to be unhealthy (see August's section, p 124). Pick your venue, get together with some friends, and enjoy an evening out.

STRESS-FREE SHOPPING

- Plan a week's menus in advance and always make a shopping list. It may take quite a time at first, but you'll get better with practice.
- Keep a 'running' shopping list and jot down store-cupboard items as you run out.
- If it's practical, do your main weekly shop alone – it can be far less stressful without 'distractions'.
- Occasionally do your main grocery shopping online and have it delivered.
- Familiarise yourself with the layout of your regular supermarket, and arrange your shopping list in aisle order.

CALMER COOKING

- Make the most of your freezer. If you're making a dish you can freeze, make a double quantity and freeze half. Then you can always give yourself an evening away from the stove by taking a main course and a dessert out of the freezer. All you need to do is prepare some fresh vegetables or a salad. You can also freeze individual portions for family members who might need to eat at unusual times, separate from the rest of the family. It's healthy convenience food – and you know what went into it.
- Most soups, stews and casseroles, cottage pies, chilli con carne (and their vegetarian versions), and Bolognese sauce can be frozen – try our Speedy Spaghetti Bolognese (page 32) made with turkey mince, which is very low in fat.
- Freeze fresh herbs, vegetables and fruits when they are in season and cheaper.
- Make a note of any days in the coming week that are going to be particularly busy or stressful. Then plan especially quick and easy meals for those days.
- Make the most of labour-saving devices like food processors and electric health grills.
- Check out the fresh-fish counter for white fish, and oily fish like salmon, sardines, and mackerel. They are delicious simply grilled with a large salad and boiled new potatoes. Fresh fish takes so little time to prepare.

Get sporty!

Use your free time to take up a new sport – remember that exercise stimulates the release of endorphins, the body's natural 'feel good' chemicals.

Take moderate exercise, at least three times a week.

Consider kick boxing, or a similar sport or martial art, if you want to work off pent-up frustration.

Or how about going for smooth and relaxing? Try t'ai chi – it's believed that the controlled and meditative moves help you to let go of your tensions.

ACTION
YOGA AND PILATES

If you don't like the spiritual dimension of many forms of yoga, you may prefer Pilates. Many Pilates instructors view it as a halfway house between relaxation and more physical workouts.

For enhancing flexibility combined with strength, yoga and Pilates are hard to beat. And both help the body and mind to cope with the stresses and strains of modern life.

Pilates is often considered more like 'exercise', but yoga is by no means a soft option – there are a huge variety of types of yoga, ranging from extremely gentle to physically demanding.

Types of yoga include:

Lyengar yoga – this stresses precision, and the alignment of the body. It may use props such as chairs and bolsters.

Viniyoga – a gentler form of yoga, tailored according to need, making it especially suitable for during pregnancy or for those suffering from a medical condition.

Ashtanga yoga – this is also known as 'power yoga'. In ashtanga you build up a sweat as you perform postures and movements in a continuous, fast style. It's physically demanding, and probably not suitable for beginners.

Pilates focuses on:

Precision – it's very important to perform the movements precisely, as you learn to isolate the various muscle groups in the body

Flowing – Pilates movements are slow and continuous

Centring – the abdominal muscles (your centre or 'core') are the key in Pilates

Breathing – correct breathing is important

Strength – by working against gravity, with perfect control, your muscles are strengthened

YOGA

Yoga offers a holistic approach to mind, body and spirit, stretching and toning every part of you. There are yoga classes available for all types – from beginners to advanced, children to seniors, yoga for pregnancy or for those with specific medical conditions.

You can buy books, videos and DVDs on yoga, but a class is probably the best way to learn the techniques safely, and many people find that the company of other like-minded souls and the support of the instructor enhance the experience.

The most commonly taught type of yoga is hatha yoga. A class generally consists of limbering postures (warm-up), asanas (postures), pranayama (breath awareness) and meditation.

PILATES

Pilates used to be the preserve of dancers, gymnasts and sportsmen and women, but now everyone can enjoy the benefits of this body-conditioning exercise.

Whether you want a flatter stomach or a stronger back, or if you just want to de-stress or recover after a sporting injury, Pilates has something to offer you. It's regarded as one of the safest exercise techniques available and lengthens and strengthens the muscles, and improves posture, without stressing the joints or the heart.

Brian Statham

Fifty-year old vicar Brian Statham wasn't just a heart attack waiting to happen – in fact he'd already had one. Brian was desperate to change his life on this earth.

But unfortunately for Brian, he was in a high risk group. He had already had one heart attack, he was male, overweight, and he ate too much salt and too many saturated fats. Plus he had a family history of heart disease. He lost both a brother and a sister to heart attacks recently and his dad also died of a heart attack – all in their 50s. Unless he radically changed his lifestyle, his life expectancy wasn't looking healthy.

The trouble was that Brian's work wasn't conducive to healthy living. His parish rounds included endless visits to local ladies who would ply him with tea and biscuits. And he drove everywhere. At five foot six Brian weighed in at an unheavenly sixteen and a half stone. That made him five stone overweight, putting an excessive strain on his already vulnerable heart.

But despite knowing he was a prime candidate for another heart attack, Brian couldn't alter his behaviour. He still stuffed himself from break of dawn to nightfall with toast and tea, biscuits and tea, cake and tea, and takeaways and tea.

Anyone who has had a heart attack is advised to cut back on three things: saturated fat, sugar and salt. Brian's consumption of salt was particularly alarming. The government recommend we should eat no more than six grams of salt a day. And the body actually only needs half a gram. Brian's daily intake was a staggering 26 grams a day. If he could reduce this intake, he would bring his blood pressure down – important for his heart and his health.

It's hardly surprising he was lacking in energy, had trouble sleeping and suffered from headaches – his tests showed he was deficient in magnesium, in vitamin B1, and thin on essential fatty acids.

So, shocked into submission, Brian took on the *You Are What You Eat* regime. His first hurdle was the idea of doing the necessary exercise, because his heart attack happened after he climbed a mountain. So to start with, he was only given gentle exercise, like walking. After a couple of weeks, though, he was given a bike and his car keys were locked in the vestry.

Four weeks into the regime and Brian began to struggle. He had a big problem with tofu, which he called the food of the devil! And his social life was suffering. It used to revolve around food and drink and he started to get very lonely on his new programme. However, when he decided to involve the rest of the parish in cooking for him and eating with him, things started to improve.

He even managed to start to wean his ladies of the parish off their traditional cake sale, getting them to swap the much-loved Victoria sponge for sugar-free, butter-free, wheat-free, chocolate-free brownies. Even 89-year-old parishioner Margaret, having initially thought it would be made of air, conceded Brian's carob fudge brownies were rather nice.

Brian kept up with a regime that helped him lose nearly two stone in eight weeks, and he felt he had learned the secret of healthy eating and exercise and had changed his destiny.

CASE STUDY

MENU PLANNER
MARCH IDEAS

MARCH BEST BUYS

Make the most of:

Broccoli
Brussels sprouts
Parsnips
Swedes
Turnips
Kale
Red Cabbage
Winter greens

Menu 1

 **Breakfast**   Breakfast buster

Lunch   Leek, pepper and pea tortilla

Dinner   Oven-roasted salmon with pesto

Griddled fruits with vanilla sauce

Menu 2

 **Breakfast**   Apple and blueberry pancakes

 Lunch   Mexican-style beanburgers

Dinner   Herby roasted lamb

Spiced oranges

Menu 1
☀ Breakfast buster

1 Place all the ingredients in a blender. Blend until smooth. Pour into tall glasses and serve. (Add extra milk or water if necessary to achieve the right consistency for drinking.)

> **Health fact:** Oat bran is rich in soluble fibre that can help regulate blood-sugar levels, thus helping sustain us between meals. It also helps reduce cholesterol levels.

200ml skimmed milk

150g fat-free bio-yogurt

6 'ready to eat' dried apricots, quartered

1 banana, peeled and cut into chunky pieces

2tbsp oat bran

1tsp clear honey

Serves 4

☀ Leek, pepper and pea tortilla

1 Thinly slice the onion, leek and pepper.
2 Heat the oil in a medium nonstick frying pan and cook the onion, leek and pepper for 4–5 minutes until softened and lightly coloured, stirring occasionally. Thinly slice the sweet potato and add to the pan. Stir in the peas and cook together for 5 minutes, turning the vegetables regularly.
3 Place the eggs, milk and a little ground black pepper in a bowl and whisk until well combined.
4 Pour the eggs over the top of the vegetables in the frying pan and cook on a low heat for 10 minutes until the eggs are almost set. Preheat the grill to hot.
5 Place the frying pan under the grill, being careful to avoid heating the handle, and cook until the egg is set and lightly browned – about 2 minutes.
6 Loosen the edges of the tortilla with a round-bladed knife and turn out onto a board. Cut into wedges. Serve hot or cold with a lightly dressed salad.

1 small onion, peeled and quartered

1 small leek, trimmed

1 red pepper, deseeded and halved

1tbsp virgin olive oil, plus extra for greasing

1 small sweet potato, peeled and quartered lengthways (about 200g peeled weight)

100g frozen peas

6 medium free-range eggs

4tbsp skimmed milk

Freshly ground black pepper

A large, lightly dressed salad, to serve

Serves 4

> **Health fact:** Sweet potatoes are excellent sources of betacarotene, a nutrient which can help protect against cancer. They also contain vitamins C and E, which help fight harmful free radicals (oxygen molecules that damage the body).

☽ Oven-roasted salmon with pesto

4 x 125g fresh salmon or other thick, firm fish fillet, skinned

Freshly ground black pepper

For the pesto:

1 small growing basil plant

75g pine nuts

1 plump garlic clove, peeled

1tbsp extra virgin olive oil

Sugar snap peas, green beans, peas and asparagus to serve

Serves 4

1 Preheat the oven to 200°C/Gas 6. Place the salmon fillets on a lightly oiled baking tray and season with freshly ground black pepper.

2 To make the pesto snip the leaves from the basil plant, reserving four sprigs for garnish if liked, and put in a food processor (you should have approximately 35g of leaves). Add the pine nuts, garlic, oil and a few twists of ground black pepper. Blend until the mixture is very finely chopped.

3 Spread a little of the pesto onto each of the fish fillets and bake for 16–18 minutes until cooked to taste. Serve with boiled new potatoes and a steamed or lightly boiled combination of sugar snap peas, green beans, peas and asparagus.

TIPS

● This salmon also tastes fantastic cooked and flaked into chunky pieces, then tossed with wholewheat spaghetti and blanched broccoli spears with a squeeze of lemon juice and lots of ground black pepper.

● Feeding fewer people? The basil pesto will keep in the fridge for up to two days. Stir a couple of tablespoons into freshly cooked wholewheat pasta or blend with low-fat bio-yogurt to make a delicious dip and serve with lots of colourful raw vegetable sticks.

Griddled fruits with vanilla sauce

25g blanched hazelnuts or almonds

Sunflower oil, for greasing

2 ripe pears, quartered and cored

2 ripe nectarines, stoned and quartered

4 ripe plums, halved and stoned

1 pot (200g) fat-free fromage frais

½ tsp vanilla extract or a few drops vanilla essence

Serves 4

1 Lightly toast the hazelnuts and almonds in a dry frying pan until they are lightly coloured. (Watch them all the time as they burn easily.)

2 Preheat a ridged griddle pan or an electric health grill and lightly oil.

3 Place the pears, nectarines and plums on the grill or griddle, and cook for 6–7 minutes until softened and lightly browned. (Close the lid if you are using an electric health grill.)

4 Mix the fromage frais with a few drops of vanilla extract.

5 Roughly chop the toasted hazelnuts or almonds.

6 Divide the fruit amongst 4 dessert plates and top with spoonfuls of fromage frais and a sprinkling of toasted nuts.

Health facts: The fruit is rich in vitamin C, which protects cells from free-radical damage and boosts immunity. The nuts provide protein, calcium and heart-healthy monounsaturated oils.

Blueberries are a rich source of vitamin C as well as powerful antioxidant phytochemicals (plant chemicals), which help protect the body from illness.

Menu 2
☀ Apple and blueberry pancakes

1 Purée the 250g blueberries with a liquidiser or stick blender and pass through a sieve to make a smooth sauce. Set aside.

2 Stir the flour, bicarbonate of soda and lemon zest together in a large bowl.

3 Make a well in the centre of the dry mixture and add the beaten eggs and buttermilk or yogurt mixture. Stir well until the batter reaches a soft, porridge-like consistency, adding 2–3tbsp water if it seems too thick.

4 Peel, quarter, core and chop the apple into small pieces – it should weigh around 150g when prepared. Stir the remaining 150g blueberries and apple into the pancake batter.

5 Heat a large nonstick frying pan gently on the hob. Drizzle a little oil into the pan and wipe around the base carefully with folded kitchen paper. Add 6 or 7 heaped teaspoonfuls of the mixture to the pan and spread gently with the back of the spoon into 6cm rounds.

6 Cook over a medium heat for 3–4 minutes. When small bubbles begin to appear on the surface of each pancake, and the edges look set, turn over and continue cooking on the other side for a further 3 minutes until both sides are golden brown.

7 Remove pancakes from the pan and sprinkle with a little of the caster sugar, if using. Keep warm while the remaining pancakes are prepared. Serve with the blueberry sauce.

TIP
● These pancakes freeze well and can be reheated from frozen. To reheat, place on a baking tray and bake in preheated oven at 190°C/Gas 5 for about 10 minutes until hot. Alternatively, allow to thaw then warm through gently in a nonstick frying pan over a low heat, turning regularly.

300g wholemeal plain flour

2tsp bicarbonate of soda

Finely grated zest of half a lemon

3 medium eggs, beaten

1 carton (284ml) buttermilk or 250g fat-free bio-yogurt mixed with 2tbsp water

1 small Bramley cooking apple

150g fresh blueberries, washed and drained

Sunflower oil, for greasing

Pinch of caster sugar, to serve (optional)

For the sauce:

250g fresh blueberries, washed

Makes 24

☼ Mexican-style bean burgers

50g brown rice

1 can (410g) 'no-salt' red kidney beans, drained and rinsed

1 small onion, peeled and quartered (about 100g prepared weight)

1 garlic clove, peeled and halved

1 small yellow pepper, deseeded and roughly chopped (about 115g prepared weight)

25g sunflower seeds

½ tsp hot chilli powder

1 bunch fresh coriander (about 15g)

Minted yogurt dip or fresh tomato salsa and a large mixed-leaf salad, to serve

Makes 8

1. Bring a medium pan of water to the boil. Add the rice and boil for 25–30 minutes, according to the directions on the pack. Drain in a sieve under running water until cold.

2. In a blender or food processor place the beans, onion, garlic, pepper, sunflower seeds, chilli powder, coriander and rice. Blend for a short time, stop and push the mixture down with a spatula.

3. Replace lid and blend until the mixture forms a thick paste (the beans and vegetables should be very finely chopped but not smooth). Remove mixture, place in a bowl and cover with clingfilm. Chill for 20 minutes.

4. Preheat the oven to 200°C/Gas 6. Line a baking tray neatly with baking parchment.

5. Using clean hands roll the bean mixture into 8 evenly sized balls. Place on the baking tray and press lightly with the back of a spoon to flatten.

6. Bake for 20–25 minutes until golden brown around the edges.

7. Leave burgers on the tray for 3–4 minutes to firm up, then carefully lift off. Serve with a yogurt dip, or fresh tomato salsa, and a large mixed-leaf salad.

Red kidney beans are low in fat and rich in slow-release carbohydrate. They provide good amounts of vitamin B1 and niacin and useful amounts of iron, which is essential for healthy red blood cells.

☽ Herby roasted lamb

1 Trim all of the fat from the lamb steaks and place them in a shallow dish. Arrange the onion rings over the meat.
2 Combine the honey, mint, mustard and vinegar in a small bowl and pour over the meat. Place the dish in the fridge for 4 hours to allow the meat to marinate. Turn once during marinating time.
3 Lift the meat out of the marinade and place in a roasting tin. The meat should be in a single layer.
4 Preheat the oven to 200°C/Gas 6 for 30 minutes or until the meat is cooked. Baste the meat with any remaining marinade during the cooking time.
5 Serve the lamb steaks with mashed or boiled potatoes and fresh seasonal vegetables.

4 lamb leg steaks

1 onion thinly sliced, and separated

2tbsp mint, finely chopped

3tbsp wine vinegar

½ tsp mild mustard (such as Dijon)

1tbsp runny honey

Freshly ground black pepper

Mashed or boiled potatoes and fresh vegetables or salad to serve

Serves 4

> **Health fact:** Lamb, like all red meats, is a good source of iron. Onions contain a substance called allicin, which can help lower levels of the 'bad' LDL cholesterol.

Spiced oranges

1 Finely grate and squeeze the juice of one of the oranges into a non-metallic bowl large enough to hold all the orange slices. Stir in the cinnamon, cloves, peppercorns and chilli flakes if liked.
2 Cut the top and base off each orange and stand upright on a board. Using a knife, carefully remove the peel and pith. Working on a large plate to catch the juices, thinly slice the oranges.
3 Stir the oranges and any of the juice caught in the plate into the spiced juice, sprinkle with pecans and serve at once spooned over frozen yogurt if liked, or cover and chill for up to 2 hours: do not add the pecans until just before serving so they don't soften.

5 medium or large oranges

½ tsp ground cinnamon

Pinch of ground cloves

4 black peppercorns, crushed with the side of a spoon

Pinch of dried chilli flakes (optional)

55g pecans, chopped

Low-fat frozen vanilla yogurt, to serve (optional)

Serves 4

april

EATING FOR ENERGY

One of the great things about healthy eating is the fact that you never need to feel hungry or skimp on portions. And eating the right kinds of foods will help keep your energy levels up throughout the day.

✓ **THIS MONTH, MAKE SURE YOU:**

- Get your finger on the pulse – increase the beans, lentils and wholegrain foods in your diet
- Eat breakfast – a healthy one every day

What about GL?

GL is an extension of the GI concept, and it stands for Glycaemic Load. As well as considering the speed with which a food raises your blood sugar, it also takes into account the amount of sugar-producing carbohydrate in a food. For example, broccoli and pasta have approximately the same GI. But a portion of broccoli contains much less carbohydrate – this means it has a lower glycaemic load, and has less of an effect on your blood sugar.

THE GLYCAEMIC INDEX

Eating nutritious food is not about deprivation – when you improve your diet, you may actually find yourself eating more food than before. The secret is to choose filling and healthy foods that sustain you between meals. The main fuel used by the body's cells is glucose – a sugar. When we eat sugar or sugary foods, it's absorbed very quickly, and needs hardly any processing before it can be used as fuel. Our blood-sugar level rises sharply, and the body thinks, 'Great – instant energy!' But all too quickly the fuel is used up or stored.

But our bodies can also obtain glucose by digesting food, absorbing it and processing it to make sugar molecules. Now let's look at what happens when we eat protein, fat or complex carbohydrates – that's the carbohydrates you find in starchy foods such as bread, rice and pasta. These require more time to be broken down, absorbed and processed by the body, so our blood sugar raises more slowly and less sharply, and the 'fuel' arrives slowly, over a longer time. Rather than getting a quick burst of energy, we feel sustained for longer.

That's the science behind the Glycaemic Index, or GI. You can buy books full of tables and figures giving GI scores for a huge range of foods and meals, or you can embark on a special GI diet.

But you don't need to worry about all of that in order to eat healthily. Simply remember a few simple GI rules and you can work it all out for yourself!

Confused about whether you're meant to go for low-GI foods or high? Remember 'low is slow' – and slow-release foods are what you want. It's the overall GI of a meal that's important, not the individual foods, so a low-GI food plus a high-GI food makes a medium-GI meal. High-fibre foods are generally low GI, and always choose 'brown' or wholemeal versions, rather than white.

Protein lowers the GI of a meal, because protein takes a long time for the body to digest and process. (Fat also lowers the GI of a meal, but you shouldn't use that as an excuse to eat foods high in saturated or trans fats, because of the health problems associated with them.)

Processing and cooking raises the GI of food, making it less effective as slow fuel. In effect, you've taken away some of the 'work' the body would have needed to do in order to digest the food. So, lightly cooked pasta and vegetables are better fuel than those that are cooked until they're soggy. They retain more nutrients too.

FILLING FIBRE

A lot of us don't get enough fibre in our diets. Fibre fills you up, and has a range of health benefits, from keeping your digestive system moving to reducing your risk of heart disease and certain cancers. Fibre-rich foods, such as wholegrains, fruit and vegetables, are also good for us in a variety of other ways, because of the vitamins, minerals and health-promoting phytochemicals (plant chemicals) they contain.

But while fibre fills us up, it doesn't fuel our bodies, and it can reduce the amount of nutrients we absorb from our diets if we rely on fibre to make us feel full. This means ultra-high fibre diets and fibre supplements aren't the best way to stop us getting peckish between meals – it's better to rely on those slow-release, low-GI fuels.

DIETING MYTHS

It's hard to find an adult who hasn't been on a weight-loss diet, and shops and the Internet are full of diets promising miraculous means of shedding pounds.

But many of these diets work only by drastically limiting the foods that are allowed, so dieters lose out on all the nutrients they contain. Even if pounds are lost initially, the diets aren't sustainable. People return to their old eating habits, and the weight creeps back.

This 'yo-yo' dieting isn't just unproductive and demoralising, it also weakens the body's natural resilience and confuses its in-built weight-stabilising mechanism.

The healthiest way to gain and maintain a lean, strong and healthy body is to eat a balanced and nutritious diet and keep active. This is a way of life, not a faddy, unsustainable flash in the pan, and the benefits will stay with you for ever.

Ignore these diet myths – they're untrue, and can be dangerous:

- **The stricter the diet, the better it will work.**
  Wrong! You'll get bored and miserable, and probably give up.
- **Very-low-calorie diets are the best way to lose weight.**
  Wrong! You'll lose out on vital nutrients, and confuse your body's natural weight-regulation mechanism.
- **If you eat few enough calories, it doesn't matter if you don't do any exercise.**
  Wrong! Exercise is important to keep your body healthy and maintain muscle.
- **You have to count calories in order to lose weight.**
  Wrong! If you need to lose weight, simply following a healthy diet will enable you to shed any excess pounds.
- **Skipping meals is a good way to lose weight.**
  Wrong! You'll be more likely to pounce on an unhealthy between-meals snack.
- **Starchy foods like bread and potatoes make you fat.**
  Wrong! Starchy foods (especially wholegrain) contain important nutrients. It's usually the fatty toppings, like butter and creamy pasta sauces, that pile on the pounds.
- **You must cut out all fat in order to lose weight.**
  Wrong! We need a certain proportion of fat in our diets, particularly the polyunsaturated fats found in oily fish, nuts and seeds (see page 112).
- **Diets based around one food (cabbage, celery, grapefruit etc.) are a good way to lose weight.**
  Wrong! You need a balanced diet to obtain all the essential nutrients from your food.

Super slow-fuel foods:

- ◆ Oats
- ◆ Brown pasta
- ◆ Brown rice
- ◆ Wholemeal bread
- ◆ Beans and lentils
- ◆ Apples and pears (tropical fruits are higher in quick-release sugar, so less effective at keeping your blood-sugar levels stable)

Concentrate on sustainable healthy eating and you'll reap lifelong benefits.

DITCH THE CARBS?
WHAT WAS THAT ALL ABOUT?

A certain low-carbohydrate, high-protein and high-fat diet has been very popular recently, probably because it encourages the foods that other weight-loss diets frown on. People did lose weight with low-carb diets, but many complained of side effects, that the diet was not sustainable, and that they were worried about the effect of all that protein and fat on their health.

There was a lot of debate on why the diet seemed to work. The general conclusion from scientists was that the high protein and fat content curbed people's appetites, so they didn't want to eat so much.

Because this kind of diet is such a new phenomenon, we don't know its long-term effects on health. But we do know that saturated fats can be harmful in large amounts, and that starchy foods and fruit contain nutrients that are essential for a healthy, balanced diet.

WHAT'S THE POINT OF POINTS?

Diets allocating 'points' to foods based on their calorie, fat and fibre content have proven successful for many people, particularly when combined with a supportive, social 'club' setting. You're given a daily points limit, and it's up to you what to 'spend' it on. Unfortunately, though, because no foods are off limits, it's possible to save your points for fatty, sugary foods, while never addressing the unhealthy food habits that make you want to eat them. And by splurging your points on less healthy foods, you lose out on the nutrients you'd get from choosing the healthier alternatives.

ACTION
GET WALKING!

Walking is the most natural form of exercise in the world. You don't need any special clothing or equipment, you can do it wherever you live and whatever your age or circumstances – all you have to do is put one foot in front of the other.

Walking can:

- Help you to get and stay fit, and tone up your muscles
- Boost your mood
- Lower blood pressure
- Reduce high cholesterol
- Reduce the risk of heart disease and stroke
- Reduce body fat
- Increase and maintain bone density, helping to prevent osteoporosis
- Help to control body weight
- Help flexibility and co-ordination

Ideally, you should incorporate thirty minutes of walking into most days. It doesn't need to be all at once. Try these tips to increase your steps – every little helps.

- Get off the bus one stop early, and walk the rest of the way to your destination
- Use the stairs instead of the lift at work
- Buy a pedometer – it's a real motivator to watch those steps accumulate
- Walk the dog – or volunteer to exercise a friend's pet
- Join a local walking club – it's a great way to make friends

Briskly does it

You should be able to just about carry out a conversation while you walk – don't amble, but don't push yourself so hard that you're panting for breath.

If you put a bit of energy into it, walking counts as aerobic exercise.

MENU PLANNER

 **APRIL BEST BUYS**

Make the most of:
Purple-sprouting broccoli
Watercress
New-season carrots
Spinach
Fennel
Leeks

Menu 1

Breakfast — Apple and raisin porridge

Lunch — Beef salad with beetroot and horseradish

Dinner — Coriander and garlic tofu

Banana and chocolate yogurt parfait

Menu 2

Breakfast — Yogurt, cereal and fruit sundae

Lunch — Steamed plaice with asparagus

Dinner — Spiced chicken with lime sauce

Poached fruit with cinnamon

Menu 1

☼ Apple and raisin porridge

1 Place the oats in a large saucepan with the water and stir. Place over a medium heat and bring to the boil, stirring all the time. Reduce the heat and simmer gently for 10 minutes, continuing to stir. Stir in as much milk as you need to reach the required consistency. Any remaining milk can be placed in a jug and served with the porridge. Pour the porridge into 4 bowls.
2 Wash the apple and roughly chop. Scatter the apple and raisins over the porridge in the bowls. Grate a little fresh nutmeg over the fruit, if liked. Drizzle with a little maple syrup or honey.

200g jumbo oats (not instant)

600ml water

400ml skimmed or semi-skimmed milk

50g raisins

2 eating apples, roughly chopped

A little grated nutmeg

Honey or maple syrup to taste

Serves 4

☼ Beef salad with beetroot and horseradish

1 Brush a nonstick frying pan with a little oil and place over a medium heat. Season the steak on both sides with ground black pepper and place in the pan. Cook for 2 minutes on each side for medium-rare meat or adjust cooking time to suit your taste. Remove from the pan and set aside to cool.
2 Wash the watercress and salad leaves under cold running water. Drain and remove excess water. Arrange the leaves on a large serving plate.
3 Bring a small pan of water to the boil and cook the mangetout for just 1 minute. Drain in a sieve under cold running water. Slice the beetroot.
4 Place beetroot slices and mangetout on top of the salad leaves.
5 Slice the steak thinly and arrange on the salad. Mix the horseradish and yogurt. Spoon the dressing over the salad. Serve with baked jacket potatoes.

½ tsp olive oil

350g lean sirloin steak, trimmed of fat

1 large bunch watercress, trimmed and tough stalks removed

4 handfuls mixed salad leaves, such as frisée, baby leaf and rocket

4 vacuum-packed, plain-cooked beetroot, drained

100g mangetout, trimmed and washed

Freshly ground black pepper

For the dressing:

4tsp hot horseradish sauce

6tbsp fat-free bio-yogurt

Serves 4

> **Health fact:** lean beef is an excellent source of the mineral iron, which is needed for the manufacture of red blood cells, as well as zinc, which is vital for a healthy immune system. The protein in beef also helps you feel sustained between meals.

☾ Coriander and garlic tofu

2 garlic cloves, crushed

2tsp finely grated fresh root ginger

4tbsp chopped fresh coriander

Finely grated zest and freshly squeezed juice of 2 limes

2 x 250g packs fresh tofu, drained

Sunflower oil, for greasing

Tamari soy sauce

Serves 4

1 Mix the garlic, ginger, coriander, lime zest and juice in a non-metallic bowl. Cut the tofu into around 20 small cubes and add to the marinade. Turn gently to coat in the marinade, then cover and leave to marinate in the fridge for 1–2 hours.

2 Lightly oil a nonstick frying pan and preheat. Lift the tofu out of the bowl, one piece at a time and place in the pan. Cook for 1½–2 minutes, turn the tofu pieces over and cook for another minute, until lightly browned on both sides. Sprinkle with soy sauce. Serve the tofu on a bed of stir-fried fresh vegetables.

Health facts: Tofu is made from soya-bean curd, and the protein in tofu may help reduce high blood-cholesterol levels. Plain tofu can taste very bland, but it soaks up the flavour of the marinade like a sponge.

Banana and chocolate yogurt parfait

50g plain chocolate (70% cocoa solids), broken into squares

3 large bananas, peeled

200g fat-free bio-yogurt

Fresh berries (such as halved strawberries, raspberries and red currants)

Fresh mint sprigs, to serve

Serves 4

1 Melt the chocolate in a bowl over a small pan of simmering water (or melt in a microwave according to the manufacturer's instructions).

2 Blend the bananas in a food processor with the yogurt until smooth. Add the chocolate in a slow, steady stream through the feed chute with the motor running.

3 Spoon the banana mixture into four plastic party cups or 150ml ramekins lined with clingfilm. Cover and freeze for 6 hours or overnight. Remove from the freezer 10–15 minutes before serving.

4 Push out of plastic cups, or turn out of ramekins and remove the clingfilm, and transfer to dessert plates. Decorate with summer berries and mint sprigs.

Menu 2

☼ Yogurt, cereal and fruit sundae

1. Into a tall glass place half of the yogurt followed by half of the cereal. Repeat the layers.
2. Top with chopped fresh, seasonal fruit.

> **Health fact:** Yogurt is a great source of calcium – a 150g pot of low-fat plain yogurt can contain over a quarter of your daily calcium requirements.

1 carton (150g) low-fat plain yogurt

1 portion low-sugar or sugar-free cereal

1 portion fresh fruit in season

Serves 1

☀ Steamed plaice with asparagus

1. Make a small slit in the side of each tomato and place in a bowl. Cover with just boiled water and stand for 2–3 minutes until skins loosen. Remove tomatoes with a slotted spoon and cool for a few minutes before peeling.
2. Cut in half and remove the seeds. Cut the tomato flesh into 1cm dice and mix with the vinegar, oil and a little ground black pepper. Set aside.
3. Fill the bottom of a steamer with water. Put the fish fillets on a board and cut in half lengthways through the middle with a sharp knife. Place 5 or 6 asparagus tips (depending on size) at the thicker end of each fillet and roll up. Sprinkle with the lemon juice and scatter the orange pepper over. Place in a dish that will fit in your steamer basket.
4. Steam for about 10 minutes until the fish and asparagus are cooked.
5. Warm the tomato dressing in a small pan over a low heat for a few seconds, stirring regularly – do not overheat.
6. Lift the fish and diced pepper carefully onto two plates and spoon over the warm tomato dressing. Serve with boiled new potatoes and seasonal vegetables or a large mixed salad.

> **Health fact:** Although white fish such as plaice only contain low levels of the heart-healthy omega-3 oils found in abundance in their oily fish cousins, they are a really low-fat source of protein.

2 fresh plaice fillets, each about 150g, skinned

100g fine asparagus tips, trimmed

1tbsp freshly squeezed lemon juice

½ a small orange pepper, deseeded and cut into 1cm dice

For the dressing:

2 large, ripe tomatoes

1tsp cider vinegar

1tbsp extra virgin olive oil

Freshly ground black pepper

Serves 4

Spiced chicken with lime sauce

4 boneless chicken breasts, preferably free range or organic, skinned

150g fat-free bio-yogurt

1tsp ground cumin

1tsp ground coriander

1tsp hot chilli powder

1tsp finely grated fresh root ginger

1 garlic clove, peeled and crushed

Sunflower oil, for greasing

For the sauce:

5tbsp fat-free bio-yogurt

1tsp mango chutney

1tsp freshly squeezed lime juice

1tbsp chopped fresh mint

Lime wedges, for squeezing

Warmed wholemeal pitta bread (or a small baked jacket potato) and a mixed leaf and tomato salad, to serve

Serves 4

1 Cut the chicken into 3cm pieces and place in a bowl. Add the yogurt, spices, ginger and garlic. Toss well together then cover and leave to marinate in the fridge for 4–6 hours.

2 Lightly oil and preheat an electric health grill or ridged griddle pan. Tip the chicken and marinade into a colander over a bowl and shake to remove most of the marinade. Place the chicken pieces on the grill or griddle and cook for 3–4 minutes. Close the lid if you are using a health grill. Turn the chicken pieces with tongs or a fork every minute if using a griddle. Cook until the chicken is cooked through and no pinkness remains.

3 To make the sweet lime sauce, mix the yogurt, chutney and lime juice together in a small bowl.

4 Serve the chicken with lime wedges for squeezing, warmed pitta bread, lots of salad and the sweet lime sauce.

> **Health fact:** Studies suggest that garlic can reduce the risk of heart attack and stroke by making the blood less sticky and less likely to clot.

Poached fruit with cinnamon

2 apples, cut into 6–8 pieces

2 oranges, halved

½ a cinnamon stick

350g mixed dried orchard fruits, such as apples, peaches, apricots, pears and plums

Fat-free bio-yogurt and roughly chopped nuts and seeds, to serve

Serves 4

1 Feed the apples through a juicer and pour into a saucepan. Juice the oranges and stir into the apple juice. Add the cinnamon stick and dried fruit to the saucepan.

2 Cook over a low heat for 10 minutes, allowing the juice to bubble gently. Remove from the heat, take out the cinnamon stick, and set aside for 5 minutes.

3 Serve the fruit warm or cold with spoonfuls of yogurt and a sprinkling of roughly chopped nuts and seeds.

> **Health fact:** Dried apricots and peaches are a good source of betacarotene, which can help protect against heart disease and cancer. it can also be converted into vitamin A in the body.

may

BE GOOD TO YOUR GUT

Now let's throw a spanner in the works – it's not as simple as saying you are what you eat. You're actually what you digest and absorb. All the nutritious food in the world won't do you a scrap of good if it goes straight through you!

If we fill up with fatty, sugary junk, and starve ourselves of nutritious food, our digestion suffers

BE GOOD TO YOUR GUT

The job of the digestive system is to take the food you give it and break it down into the raw materials for making new cells, plus energy to fuel every process in the body, from moving our muscles and pumping our blood to breathing in and out, and even thinking (the brain is a very energy-hungry organ!).

When our bodies are functioning smoothly, the digestive system can do its job as it should. But when we fill our stomachs with fatty, sugary junk, and starve ourselves of good, nutritious food, our digestion is thrown out of kilter. Add our busy lifestyles and overload of chronic stress into the equation, and things begin to go wrong.

And when something goes awry with our digestive system, we soon know about it, in a variety of ways:

- Heartburn
- Stomach upsets
- Irritable bowel syndrome
- Wind
- Constipation
- Diarrhoea

'Poorly' digestion can make us truly miserable. Not only do we suffer the obvious and unpleasant symptoms, our bodies can become deficient in vital nutrients as our digestive system is prevented from doing its job effectively.

Problems with the digestive system are one of the most common causes of ill health in this country. The good news is that prevention is largely in our hands.

If you suffer persistently from any of the conditions listed here then you should consult your doctor.

Expecting heartburn

During pregnancy, the growing baby can press upwards on the stomach, causing acid to leak out of the top of the stomach. The effects of the female hormone progesterone during pregnancy also temporarily weakens the valve keeping the stomach closed.

HEARTBURN

A burning feeling behind the breastbone, or an acidic sensation that bubbles up from the stomach into the throat, heartburn is the commonest form of indigestion. The muscular ring that keeps the top of the stomach closed relaxes momentarily, allowing the stomach's acidic contents to flow back into the gullet, and sometimes even the mouth, where we experience it as a burning, acidic taste.

The stomach lining is designed to resist acidity, with a thick, mucus-covered coating. But the gullet has no such protection – hence the pain.

How diet can help heartburn:

- Don't overeat – heavy meals can lead to indigestion and heartburn. It's your stomach's way of telling you you've overdone things!
- Take time to enjoy your meals – slowly. If you gobble your food, you won't chew it properly, and chewing is important to get the digestive process off to a good start. Unchewed chunks of food have to stay longer in the stomach, being churned around and broken up by digestive enzymes. And the longer food remains in the stomach, the more food builds up, as the digestive system won't allow it to leave until it's good and ready! This means that the stomach becomes overfull, increasing the likelihood of heartburn.
- Eat little and often. If you skip meals and then gorge yourself, your stomach is more likely to become overloaded, which can force open the stomach valve and cause heartburn.
- Know your triggers. Fatty foods are notorious for relaxing the stomach valve, causing heartburn, as are coffee, alcohol, onions and garlic, or very spicy foods – especially if you're not used to them. Different people have different trigger foods. You'll learn what to avoid if you're sensitive to any of them!
- Go easy on fat, especially if it's combined with spicy 'trigger foods'. If you're prone to heartburn, spicy, oily curries can be a recipe for digestive disaster!
- Don't eat too late – if you lie down soon after eating, stomach acid can 'escape' back into the gullet. If you must have a bedtime snack, make it something light, such as a yogurt, or a mug of hot milk and some oatcakes.

IRRITABLE BOWEL SYNDROME (IBS)

IBS is a painful and distressing condition, which affects up to one in five of us during our lives. It's twice as common in women than men, and often strikes between the ages of twenty and thirty.

In IBS, the gut becomes oversensitive, and its normal functioning and the movement of food through the digestive system is disrupted, causing the gut to go into spasms.

The symptoms include:
  Pain in the abdomen
  Bloating, gurgling in the stomach, and wind
  Nausea
  Constipation, diarrhoea, or alternation between the two
  Having to rush to the toilet urgently
  Lethargy and headaches

Unfortunately, IBS is proving a very difficult condition for scientists and doctors to unravel, and there is no specific 'cure'. A variety of treatments may be recommended to ease the symptoms, including anti-spasmodic drugs, painkillers and mild antidepressants (because of the brain-body connection associated with IBS).

IBS is proving a very difficult condition for scientists and doctors to unravel, and there is no specific 'cure'.

- Banish the frying pan – switch to low fat cooking methods
- Get the hydration habit – drink plenty of water

Thinking about food

Our brains, and the way we think and feel, have a big effect on our digestion.

When we see or smell food, our mouths water as saliva flows, and our stomachs begin producing acid and enzymes ready to break down food. Our brains are sending a message that food is on the way. And the food doesn't even have to be real to elicit that 'readying' response – think how your mouth can water and your stomach gurgle at the mere *thought* of a delicious meal!

This is what happens when everything is functioning properly. But when powerful emotions come into play, when we're excited, worried or stressed, the brain's messages become confused. Our stomachs leap and churn, we feel sick and queasy. We may even suffer from stomach upsets or diarrhoea.

Stress and emotional upset is found to play a large part in a lot of cases of IBS, and many sufferers find that relieving their stress is the best way of treating their condition – relaxation, meditation, Pilates and yoga have all proven helpful. Although public awareness of IBS is increasing, sufferers may feel that no one understands what they're going through, and suffer from feelings of loneliness. If you suffer from IBS, you should try to avoid worrying about it, since this could make your condition even worse. Instead, contact a self-help or support group, who will understand and be able to supply you with information and help you through your symptoms.

In some cases, diet appears to play a role in triggering IBS, so sufferers are generally advised to keep a 'food diary' to see whether a particular food sets them off. Then the offending food or foods can be avoided.

Other dietary changes that might help include:

- Cutting out any 'trigger foods' (but be careful not to cut out too many without taking nutritional advice, as you may be losing out on vital nutrients).
- Eating smaller, more frequent meals.
- Gradually increasing the amount of fibre eaten. But avoid the temptation to sprinkle wheat bran on your food, as this can irritate the gut.
- Drinking plenty of water, diluted fruit juice, and fruit and herb teas. Limit your intake of coffee and regular tea, and avoid fizzy drinks.

WIND

Wind is something we don't like to talk about! Gases build up in the digestive system, causing an uncomfortable build-up of pressure. The only way to relieve the discomfort is for the gases to be expelled at one end or the other – which can prove embarrassing!

There are various dietary causes of wind – if you recognise any of these in yourself, modify your diet and see if this helps:

- Swallowing air while eating – although dinner table conversation is only to be encouraged, try not to chatter nineteen-to-the-dozen when you eat. Eating on the move also encourages air swallowing – so munching a sandwich while walking down the street is not a good idea!
- Chewing gum – this also encourages air swallowing. Go easy on the gum if you think it gives you wind.
- Fizzy drinks – it's obvious that those gases you're guzzling have got to go somewhere!
- Large quantities of high-fibre foods (beans are notorious!) can trigger a gas build-up in the gut. Soaking dried beans overnight before cooking, then discarding the soaking water, can help reduce their wind-producing properties. If you're making the effort to increase your fibre intake, do it gradually. This gives your intestine time to adapt to processing the extra fibre.
- Not chewing your food properly can also encourage wind.

CONSTIPATION

Constipation can make you feel truly miserable, but can usually be treated and prevented with simple diet and lifestyle changes. The following tips should help:

- Lack of fluids can cause constipation. Drink plenty of fluids, especially water, fruit juice, herb and fruit teas.
- As well as providing valuable fluids, pure fruit juice also helps prevent and relieve constipation.
- Eat prunes – they really do work! And if you need any more reason to munch on these sweet and tasty dried plums, they're also packed full of health-promoting antioxidants.
- Eat at least five portions of fruit and vegetables per day.
- Exercise – physical activity encourages the normal healthy movement of food through the digestive system.

Although these simple measures might be enough to prevent you from becoming 'blocked up', there are other causes for becoming constipated, such as pregnancy, and the side effects of some prescription medicines.

KEEPING YOUR BACTERIA BLOOMING

Bacteria are very trendy at the moment. We're all being encouraged to boost the 'friendly bacteria' that live inside us, and the adverts promise amazing benefits from these beneficial bugs.

But just what are friendly bacteria, why do we need them, and do they really work?

PROBIOTICS

Each of us has around one hundred trillion bacteria (that's a one followed by fourteen zeros) living inside our bodies. Four hundred bacteria species live naturally inside our guts, and far from being harmful, most of them are positively useful, aiding digestion, helping to nourish the cells of the gut wall, boosting immunity and producing important vitamins and minerals. These beneficial bugs are our 'friendly bacteria'.

Unfortunately, there are some bad bugs in there too. When we're healthy and well nourished, the good bacteria have the upper hand, but people are now concerned that our modern diets and lifestyles – stress, processed foods, chemicals, more use of antibiotics – are cramping the friendly bacteria's style, suppressing their growth and allowing the harmful bugs to flourish. And many people believe that when the bad bacteria crowd out the good ones, a whole host of ailments are the result, including headaches, chronic fatigue, and digestive problems such as IBS.

Probiotics aim to boost the 'friendly' bacteria in our gut.

All about fibre

Most of us don't eat enough fibre. The recommended amount is 18g per day, but most of us consume only two-thirds of this. There are two kinds of fibre:

Insoluble fibre: This is good for our digestive systems. It absorbs water and 'bulks up' the food in our gut, giving our intestines something to work on and keeping food moving smoothly through the digestive tract. It's found in foods such as wholemeal bread, brown rice, wholemeal pasta and other wholegrains, fruit and vegetables (especially their skins).

Soluble fibre: This kind of fibre lowers our levels of the harmful kind of cholesterol, and also helps keep our blood-sugar levels stable. It's found in some beans and pulses, and some fruits and vegetables (apples are especially good) and is the kind of fibre that makes oats sticky!

Oats are great for fibre – yet another reason to eat your porridge.

Enter the probiotics! These are the little bottles of milky drinks, certain 'live' yogurts, capsules and powders, containing doses of live friendly bacteria for us to swallow, to top up our delightfully named 'beneficial gut flora'.

The idea is that the bacteria join their cousins in our intestines, where they flourish, boosting the 'friendly' population. The problem is the route they have to take to arrive at their new home.

When we swallow probiotic friendly bacteria, they have to pass through the stomach, which is extremely acidic. Many scientists believe that, by the time they arrive in the lower reaches of the gut, almost all of the probiotic bacteria will have been killed.

Nevertheless, many people whose gut bacteria balance has been disrupted (for example, by taking antibiotics, which kill bacteria, the good ones included) have experienced good results from taking probiotics.

So, for now, the jury is out regarding probiotics. In theory, they're a great idea, if we can ensure that we can get them safely to the bowel where they're needed. But for healthy people, eating a balanced diet, they probably won't provide any visible health benefits.

PREBIOTICS

Recently, another player has entered the story – the confusingly named prebiotics. Unlike the probiotics, these are not live bacteria. Prebiotics are 'bacteria food', but only the beneficial bacteria can use them.

The argument for prebiotics runs like this: if we can't get live friendly bacteria into the bowel, why not feed and encourage the ones that are already living there?

We can't digest prebiotics, so they pass unaltered through our stomachs, to join the bacteria in our bowels. And the results are very encouraging, so much so that we're seeing prebiotics being added to a variety of products, from yogurt drinks to breakfast cereals. You can also buy prebiotics in capsules and powders.

Top tips – eating for healthy digestion

- Eat plenty of fruits and vegetables – they contain insoluble fibre, which helps keep your intestines moving smoothly, as well as other compounds that act as natural laxatives.
- Switch to wholemeal – eat wholemeal bread, wholemeal pasta, brown rice and other wholegrains, for their higher insoluble fibre content.
- Drink more – insufficient fluid intake can lead to constipation. Drinking enough is particularly important if you're increasing your fibre intake.
- Don't rush your meals – sit down, chew properly and take time to enjoy your food.
- Cut out or cut down on alcohol, coffee and fizzy drinks. Avoid very spicy foods if they are a 'trigger' for you.
- Try to relax – stress is involved in many digestive problems.

ACTION
AEROBIC EXERCISE

If you thought aerobic exercise was all about studios full of lithe young things leaping around in Lycra, think again!

Although aerobics classes do count as a form of aerobic exercise, there are plenty of other ways to gain the undeniable health benefits of this form of activity.

When you exercise aerobically, your cardiovascular system – your heart, lungs and blood vessels – really benefit. As you exercise, your heart beats more strongly, your pulse speeds up, you breathe more deeply, and oxygenated blood courses around your body. Regular aerobic exercise, over time, will improve the performance of your heart and lungs, and increase the oxygen supply available to your body.

The heart is a muscular organ, and as it's exercised, it grows stronger. But, like other muscles, you have to be careful not to put undue stress on the heart, by exercising beyond its capabilities.

For this reason, you should exercise so that your heart rate stays within your target zone – that's between sixty and eighty per cent of your theoretical maximum heart rate (see right). Take your pulse while you're exercising, to check how you're doing. If your pulse rate is below your target heart-rate zone, you won't be receiving aerobic benefits from your exercise, and if it rises above your target zone, this could be dangerous.

Here are some aerobic ideas to get you going:

Walking
Cycling
Jogging
Swimming
Skiing
Aerobic classes or videos
Plus any other classes that get your heart rate into its target zone – try aquarobics, kick boxing, trampolining, racket sports, or team sports.

Safety first

You should always warm up before any kind of exercise, and cool down afterwards, to avoid injuring yourself. If any of these exercises are new to you then consult your GP before beginning an exercise programme.

Find your target heart-rate zone:

- Subtract your age from 220. The number you get represents your theoretical maximum heart rate.

- Multiply your theoretical maximum by 0.6 to get your lower (60%) figure

- Multiply your theoretical maximum by 0.8 to get your higher (80%) figure

- In order for your aerobic exercise to be effective, you need to be working in your target heart-rate zone for between 15 and 45 minutes. If you find it hard going at first, stay in the lower end of your zone.

MAY BEST BUYS

Make the most of:

Raspberries

Rhubarb

New potatoes

Watercress

Purple sprouting broccoli

Cauliflower

Carrots

Fennel

Leeks

Menu 1

☀ **Breakfast**   Beans on toast with a poached egg

☼ **Lunch**   Salmon houmous with rye bread and salad

☾ **Dinner**   Red lentil and nut loaf

Frozen berry granita

Menu 2

☀ **Breakfast**   Citrus fruit salad with yogurt

☼ **Lunch**   Spiced veggie burgers with avocado and tomato lime salsa

☾ **Dinner**   Roasted fish with a crumb topping and yogurt sauce

Creamy orange jelly

Menu 1

☼ Beans on toast with a poached egg

1 Put the beans into a small saucepan and warm.
2 Toast the bread.
3 Into a frying pan, pour 4cm of boiling water. Add 1tsp vinegar, and simmer gently.
4 Break each egg and slip into the water. Cook until the white is set.
5 Put each slice of toast on a plate, pour some of the beans onto each slice, and top with the poached eggs. Sprinkle with pepper, if liked.

1 large tin no-sugar baked beans

4 slices wholemeal bread

4 eggs

Freshly ground black pepper, to taste

Serves 4

> **Health fact:** A small tin of baked beans counts as one portion towards your minimum 'five-a-day' servings of fruit and vegetables.

☀ Salmon houmous with rye bread

1 Remove any skin from the salmon and place the salmon into a blender or food processor with the water, chickpeas, garlic and tahini. Blend until smooth. Tip into a bowl and season with pepper. Cover and chill until ready to serve.
2 To make the salad: Place the mixed salad leaves on 4 plates. Arrange the other ingredients over the leaves. Combine the balsamic vinegar and olive oil in a ramekin and drizzle over the salad.
3 Place spoonfuls of the salmon mixture beside the salad on the plates. Serve with rye bread.

2 small tins (2 x 105g approx.) red salmon

1 can (400g) chickpeas, drained and rinsed

3 cloves garlic

4tbsp tahini (sesame seed paste)

Freshly ground black pepper.

1–2tbsp water

4–6 wholemeal pitta breads, toasted

For the salad:

A few handfuls of mixed salad leaves

One bunch radishes, thinly sliced

1 large carrot, grated

2 tomatoes, sliced

1 small red onion, finely sliced

¼ cucumber, sliced

1tbsp balsamic vinegar

1tbsp olive oil

Serves 4

> **Health fact:** Eat the soft, cooked bones in the tinned salmon along with the flesh – they're rich in calcium, which is essential for healthy bones.

☾ Red lentil and nut loaf

2tsp virgin olive oil, plus extra for greasing

1 medium onion, peeled and finely chopped

2 garlic cloves, peeled and crushed

3 medium carrots, peeled and diced (about 150g prepared weight)

2 medium leeks, trimmed and thinly sliced (about 200g prepared weight)

200g split red lentils, rinsed in a sieve under cold running water

600ml cold water

2tsp organic vegetable bouillon (stock) powder

85g shelled whole Brazil nuts

85g blanched almonds

1 medium free-range egg, beaten

40g fresh wholegrain breadcrumbs

2tbsp chopped fresh parsley

85g soft mild goats' cheese

Freshly ground black pepper

Makes 8 slices

1 Heat the oil in a large saucepan and gently fry the onion, garlic, carrots and leeks for 7–8 minutes until softened, stirring regularly. Add the lentils and cook with the vegetables for 30 seconds before adding the water and stock powder.

2 Bring to the boil, then reduce the heat and simmer gently for about 20 minutes until the lentils are very soft and all the water has been absorbed – it should have a thick, porridge-like consistency. Skim off any foam that rises to the surface and stir regularly, especially towards the end, so that the lentils don't stick.

3 Lightly oil a 900g nonstick loaf tin and line the base with baking parchment. Roughly chop a quarter of the nuts and finely chop the rest. Preheat the oven to 190°C/Gas 5. Stir the egg into the vegetable and lentil mixture, followed by the breadcrumbs, nuts, parsley and a few twists of ground black pepper.

4 Spoon half the mixture evenly into the loaf tin. Break the goats' cheese into pieces and scatter on top. Finish with the remaining lentil mixture. Smooth the surface with a spoon and bake for about 45 minutes until the loaf is set and lightly browned. Cover the tin loosely with foil if the loaf begins to over-brown.

5 Remove the tin carefully from the oven and cool for 5 minutes before loosening the edges of the loaf with a round-ended knife and turning out. Serve hot or cold, in slices, with a lightly dressed salad or freshly cooked vegetables.

> **Health fact:** Red lentils contain a great balance of protein and complex carbohydrates, plus soluble fibre, and provide sustained energy.

Frozen berry granita

500g frozen mixed berries, such as blueberries, redcurrants, raspberries and strawberries

About 4tbsp orange juice

Up to 1tbsp clear honey (optional)

Serves 4

1 Put the berries, straight from the freezer, and orange juice into a food processor or heavy-duty blender. Blend until the fruit is well broken up and fine ice crystals form.

2 Add honey to taste and quickly blend again, then serve at once.

Red and purple fruits, such as berries, are packed with anti-oxidants called anthocyanins. Buying them frozen is a good way to enjoy the taste and benefits of these superfoods year round, as freezing preserves the nutrients in the berries.

Avocados are an excellent source of vitamin E, which also keeps the heart healthy.

Menu 2
☀ Citrus fruit salad with yogurt

1 Skin the grapefruit and oranges and remove the flesh.
2 Chop the nuts and lightly toast the oats in a dry saucepan. Make sure they do not burn.
3 Take 4 tall glasses and place half of the fruit in the base. Add half of the yogurt, then the remainder of the fruit followed by the rest of the yogurt. Top with the toasted nuts and oats.

> **Health fact:** Brazil nuts are a brilliant source of the mineral selenium, which helps support the immune system.

1 ruby grapefruit

2 oranges

200ml low-fat yogurt

2tbsp chopped hazelnuts and Brazil nuts

2tbsp toasted oats

Serves 4

☀ Spiced veggie burgers

1 Preheat the oven to 200°C/Gas 6. Line a large baking tray neatly with baking parchment. Place all the burger ingredients in a food processor and blend for 10 seconds.
2 Remove the lid and push the mixture down with a spatula. Blend once or twice more until fairly smooth but thick enough to form a ball. Do not over-blend. Remove the blade and, using clean hands, shape the mixture into 12 balls – each about the size of a golf ball. Place on the prepared tray.
3 Flatten the balls slightly with the back of a spoon and bake for 20–25 minutes until golden around the edges. Cool for 2–3 minutes, and then lift carefully off the tray.
4 To make the salsa, put all of the prepared salsa ingredients into a bowl. Mix to combine. Leave for 30 minutes for the flavours to infuse. Serve with the burgers.
5 Serve two or three burgers as a serving, either hot or cold with an avocado salsa, or minted yogurt dip, and a large colourful salad.

TIP

● The cooked burgers can be frozen for up to a month, so you could make a double quantity and have them ready for quick meals or lunch boxes. To reheat the burgers bake thoroughly from frozen at 200°C/Gas 6 for 10–12 minutes or until hot.

1 can (410g) 'no-salt' chickpeas, drained and rinsed under cold running water

1 carrot, peeled and coarsely grated (about 75g prepared weight)

1 medium onion, peeled and chopped (about 125g prepared weight)

50g pine nuts

2tbsp tahini (sesame seed paste), measured after oil is drained

1 fat garlic clove, peeled and halved

1 bunch fresh coriander (about 20g)

Finely grated zest of half a lemon

2tsp ground cumin

For the avocado and lime salsa:

Half a stoned and peeled avocado

2 tomatoes, chopped

Half a red onion, finely chopped

2tbsp fresh coriander, chopped

Juice and finely grated zest of 1 lime

Serves 4

☾ Roasted fish with a crumb topping and yogurt sauce

1 medium slice wholegrain bread, cut into four pieces

15g pine nuts

Small bunch fresh parsley

4 x 140g thick fish fillets, such as cod, haddock or salmon, skinned

Olive oil, for greasing

Small bag of spinach, watercress and rocket salad

150g fat-free bio-yogurt

12 cherry tomatoes, halved

A third of a cucumber, sliced

1 small red, yellow or orange pepper, deseeded and sliced

Serves 4

1 Preheat the oven to 200°C/Gas 6. Using a food processor blend the bread, pine nuts and parsley, until the herbs are finely chopped and the bread is crumbed. Remove the blade and wash the bowl.

2 Place the fish fillets on a lightly oiled baking tray. Spoon the breadcrumb mixture on top of each one and press down lightly with your fingertips. Bake for 12–15 minutes until the fish is cooked and the crumb topping is golden.

3 While the fish is cooking, make the sauce. In the food processor place a handful of the spinach, watercress and rocket salad, and pour over the yogurt. Pulse until the leaves are very finely chopped, removing the lid and pushing down the mixture with a spatula once or twice.

4 Toss the remaining leaves with the tomatoes, cucumber and pepper.

5 Serve the fish hot with the yogurt sauce, boiled new potatoes and a mixed leaf salad.

Creamy orange jelly

25fl.oz freshly squeezed orange juice

2tbsp caster sugar

2 sachets of gelatine or agar-agar

7tbsp fromage frais

Serves 4

1 Pour 120ml pure orange juice into a saucepan. Sprinkle in the gelatine or agar-agar. Stir over a low heat until warm and the setting agent has dissolved. Remove from the heat as soon as the setting agent has dissolved – do not let it come to the boil.

2 Add the sugar and stir until it has dissolved. Pour in the remaining juice. Transfer to a large bowl and chill in the fridge until thickened and beginning to set around the edge of the bowl.

3 Whisk the jelly until fluffy and smooth. Whisk in the fromage frais, pour into a mould and chill overnight.

4 Serve the jelly on a plate surrounded by mandarin orange segments or fresh berries.

Health fact: Fromage frais is a good source of bone-strengthening calcium. Research suggests that achieving optimal calcium intake may also help with weight control and reducing high blood pressure.

Cherry tomatoes are even richer in nutrients than their larger relatives. They're great for vitamin C and E, plus betacarotene and the plant chemical lycopene.

june

DEFENDING YOUR BODY – WITH FOOD

At this very moment, we're under attack! Every minute of the day, we are constantly bombarded with millions of viruses and bacteria, while at the same time being assaulted by allergens such as certain foods and dust.

Immunity quiz

- Do you suffer from a lot of minor infections?
- Does your skin take a long time to heal?
- Do you smoke?
- Do you spend time in a smoky atmosphere most days?
- Do you live in a polluted environment?
- Do you eat fried food most days?
- Do you eat fewer than two portions of fruit a day?
- Do you eat fewer than three portions of vegetables a day?
- Do you rarely eat (unsalted) nuts and seeds every day?

All of these things either indicate an immune system that's below par, or sap the effectiveness of your immune system.

The more 'yes' answers, the more important it is for you to boost your immunity with antioxidant-rich foods.

✔ THIS MONTH, MAKE SURE YOU:

- Eat 5-a-day – at least five portions of fruit and vegetables
- Maximise the amount of fresh food in your diet

THE IMMUNE SYSTEM

When germs enter the body and multiply, our immune system springs into action, to fight off the threat before it takes hold and makes us ill. And the best thing we can do to keep ourselves healthy and minimise allergies is support our immune systems and keep them strong.

There are three main players in the story:
- Germs, allergens and other 'attackers'
- Stress – an immune weakener
- Good nutrition – an immune booster

If we're poorly nourished, our immune system is weakened, so it's easier for the germs to gain a foothold, and we're more likely to fall ill. But if we're well nourished, our immune system is strengthened, enhancing our body's defences.

ATTACK OF THE FREE RADICALS

Our bodies are constantly under fire from harmful substances called 'free radicals', produced naturally in the course of everyday life, though factors such as smoking, pollution, burned or charred food, and exposure to sunlight can accelerate their production. The free radicals damage body cells – they are implicated in a whole host of health problems, from heart disease and stroke, to cancer. They're even involved in ageing and wrinkles!

Our allies in the face of this assault are the antioxidants, which can neutralise free radicals before they cause any harm. They also help lower our levels of the 'bad' LDL kind of cholesterol, reducing our risk of heart disease and stroke.

Antioxidants also protect the immune system, helping it to keep us healthy – the cells of the immune system are particularly vulnerable to damage from free radicals.

EATING FOR IMMUNITY

By ensuring that our diets are packed full of antioxidants, we can keep our body levels of these important nutrients topped up.

Antioxidants include:
- The ACE vitamins – A, C and E
- Zinc and selenium – both minerals
- Carotenoids – these include betacarotene, and are found in dark green, yellow, orange and red fruits and vegetables
- Anthocyanins found in red and purple fruits
- Catechins found in tea
- Polyphenols found in chocolate, especially dark chocolate, and red wine

FABULOUS PHYTOCHEMICALS

Fruits and vegetables – is there no end to their amazing properties? They're low in calories, their fat content is low or nonexistent, they're a great source of vitamins and minerals, and a useful boost to our fibre intake.

But just as important – and perhaps even more important – are the plant chemicals, called phytochemicals, that they contain.

So, what do phytochemicals do, and where can we find them?

- **Flavonoids** – powerful antioxidants. They include the flavones found in apple skins, onions, broccoli, grapes and olives, and flavanones, found in citrus fruits.
- **Carotenoids** – powerful antioxidants. The body can also convert betacarotene (one of the carotenoids) into vitamin A. At least forty carotenoids have been found in foods, and the best way of maximising your intake is to eat plenty of fruits and vegetables – especially the red, orange, yellow and green ones.
- **Lycopene** – an even more potent antioxidant than betacarotene. It's also linked with a reduction in prostate cancer risk. The best source of lycopene is tomatoes, but it's also found in pink grapefruits and apricots.
- **Lutein** – a carotenoid important in eye health. It's found in green leafy vegetables, and orange or yellow fruits and vegetables.
- **Phyto-oestrogens** – these plant oestrogens were given their name because of their similarity to human oestrogens. Scientific studies suggest that phyto-oestrogens could help relieve menopausal symptoms (see more in July's chapter), as well as helping to prevent heart disease. The main sources of phyto-oestrogens are soya products, but they are also found in flaxseeds, sunflower seeds, pumpkin seeds, sesame seeds, lentils and chickpeas.

MULTICOLOURED MUNCHING

Unsure which are the best fruits and vegetables to eat if you want to boost your immunity? Go for the colourful ones, and try to eat a rainbow-full of them!

Different-coloured fruits contain different antioxidants, which enhance each others' effects, and by eating a wide variety you'll be getting as many as possible.

Stuck for ideas? Try:

Red – strawberries, cherries, red peppers. Great for betacarotene and vitamin C.
Orange – sweet potatoes, carrots, orange peppers, oranges, melon. Vitamin C and betacarotene again, plus vitamin E in sweet potatoes.
Yellow – yellow peppers. Good sources of carotenoids.
Green – dark green vegetables, such as spinach, kale and broccoli, are the best sources of green antioxidants.
Blue – blueberries. Packed full of antioxidants called anthocyanins.
Purple – red grapes. More anthocyanins.

Vitamin A – for anti-infection

When vitamin A was first discovered, it was nicknamed 'the anti-infection agent'. One of the ways it protects us is by maintaining our skin and the linings of our nose, mouth, throat, digestive tract and lungs – which together provide our main barrier against germs getting inside our system.

There are two ways in which we can get vitamin A from food. Preformed vitamin A, or retinol, is found in animal sources, such as lean meat, and especially liver. But our bodies can also make vitamin A from some of the carotenoids (mainly betacarotene – which is an excellent antioxidant and free-radical zapper in its own right).

Caution: Vitamin A is stored in the body, so it's possible for toxic levels to build up if your intake is too high over a long period of time. If you eat a normal, healthy diet, you shouldn't need to worry about your vitamin A levels rising too high, unless you eat a lot of liver (the richest vitamin A source). However, some vitamin supplements can contain high doses of this vitamin, which could tip you over into the potentially dangerous zone. If in doubt, ask your pharmacist or doctor if the amount of vitamin A in a supplement is 'high'.

Zinc

Zinc is the most important mineral for immunity – if you're deficient, your body's defences will be below par. When manufactured food is processed, its zinc content is drastically reduced – yet another reason to prepare more of your meals yourself.

Vitamin E and vitamin C – teamwork in action

Vitamin E and vitamin C work together. Vitamin E is a powerful antioxidant, which is especially effective in those parts of the body where large amounts of oxygen are present, such as the lungs and the red blood cells. Vitamin E mops up those damaging free radicals, but as it does so it becomes damaged, and can act as a free radical itself. Fortunately vitamin C can spring into action and save the day, 'recycling' the vitamin E and restoring it to its protective role.

So as well as making sure you're getting enough vitamin E, you also need an adequate intake of vitamin C to recycle it (and remember that vitamin C also acts as an antioxidant in its own right). Think 'nuts and seeds, fruits and veggies'.

Take time for tea

Tea is definitely a health food! Not only is it a relaxing hot drink, it helps make your blood less 'sticky', lowering your risk of heart disease and stroke. It also acts as a powerful antioxidant, supporting your immune system, and could even act as an antiseptic, helping to prevent gum disease.

The best effects have been found in 'green' tea. Although 'ordinary' tea does contain beneficial amounts of antioxidants, you should drink it in moderation. And it's best to take your tea black, since milk binds with the antioxidants and makes them harder to absorb.

Try not to drink tea with meals, as it hinders absorption of several vitamins and minerals.

IMMUNE-BOOSTING SUPERFOODS

- **Kiwi fruits** – these fabulous furries contain almost twice as much vitamin C as oranges, and more fibre than apples.
- **Broccoli** – a rich source of carotenoids, especially betacarotene. Population studies also suggest that the phytochemicals found in broccoli (and other members of the cabbage family) can help protect against cancer, especially bowel cancer.
- **Tomatoes** – an excellent source of antioxidants, especially the carotenoids betacarotene and lycopene. Tomatoes are also a good source of vitamins C and E.
- **Carrots** – another excellent source of betacarotene. Choose the darkest orange roots for the best nutritional content.
- **Mangoes** – these luxuriously sweet tropical fruit are rich in a whole range of antioxidants. Just one mango enables you to reach your minimum vitamin C requirement for the day. A single mango also give you two-thirds of your daily dose of vitamin A and nearly half of your vitamin E. Mangoes are a valuable source of fibre, too.
- **Peppers** – as sweet peppers ripen, changing colour from green, through orange to red, their vitamin C content rises – a red pepper contains approximately three times more vitamin C than a green one. As well as containing betacarotene, peppers are also good sources of other flavonoids, such as lutein.
- **Sweet potatoes** – these are packed full of antioxidant carotenoids, such as betacarotene. They're also a useful source of vitamin E, starch and a little protein. The starch they contain makes sweet potatoes more filling than most other vegetables.
- **Almonds** – almonds are rich in the antioxidant vitamin E. They're also high in protein. Although nuts are relatively high in fat, it's the 'good' polyunsaturated variety.
- **Pumpkin seeds and sunflower seeds** – these crunchy little treats are a great source of the mineral zinc, which is important for a healthy immune system. They also pack a hefty protein punch.

As a rule, it's best to get your antioxidants from your diet, rather than from supplements. While keeping your levels of vitamins, minerals and phyto-chemicals topped up by eating plenty of antioxidant-rich foods is definitely a good thing, several antioxidants, such as vitamins A and E, zinc and selenium, can be toxic when taken in excess. It's hard to overdose on vitamins and minerals eaten in food, but far easier to take too much in supplement form.

Also, many of the antioxidants work together in complex ways that scientists still don't fully understand, and antioxidant-rich foods harness these nutritious interactions in a way that cannot be bottled!

JUNE JAMBOREE

June brings an explosion of fresh vegetables and home-grown fruit to the shops and gives us endless opportunities to prepare quick, simple, fresh meals for all the family. If you have any growers offering 'Pick Your Own' near you, take advantage of them and take the children along too – it's surprising how much more delicious a just-picked strawberry, or a pea straight from the pod, tastes, particularly if you've picked it yourself. Also check out the farmers' markets – the stalls will be filled with freshly picked vegetables and fruit.

ENEMIES OF STRONG IMMUNITY:

- **Stress** – chronic stress has been found to suppress levels of immune T-cells, and hinder the production of antibodies, putting us more at risk from infection.
- **Pollution** – if you smoke, try to quit now! And avoid smoky atmospheres if you're a non-smoker – cigarettes are the main 'pollutant' that is within our control. The good news is that you'll experience the benefits quickly – within thirty days of stopping smoking, your immune system will be stronger. Other pollutants, such as traffic fumes, and the chemicals given off by office machinery, can weaken the immune system, too.
- **Tiredness** – physical tiredness can hinder our immune response. Deep sleep stimulates a hormone that boosts immunity, while a few bad nights' sleep can hamper our immune system.
- **Overexertion** – while exercise is generally good for us, long periods of intense exertion actually weakens our immunity. Don't work out to the point of exhaustion!
- **Hygiene** – too little or too much. Cleanliness is obviously important in preventing disease, but, surprisingly, a sterile environment isn't the healthiest thing for our immune systems. People who have a little exposure to everyday dirt and germs have stronger immunity – the constant low-grade stimulation of the immune system helps keep it on top form. Children who grow up in households with pets, and where they are allowed to play outdoors, have also been found to suffer less from allergies – yet more evidence that while hygiene is vitally important for children, wrapping them up in cotton wool is not the answer. The motto here is 'hygienic, but not paranoid'.

Vitamin C for colds?

Do vitamin C tablets stop you from catching colds? Unfortunately not. But they could help you recover a little more quickly. If you take a vitamin C supplement while you actually have a cold, you could knock a couple of days off the duration of your illness.

You can also boost your vitamin C intake by eating fruits such as oranges and other citrus fruits, and making a soothing drink from fresh orange juice and hot water.

Berry good

Make the most of the summer red berries when they are in season. Mix 750g washed berries – strawberries, raspberries, blackberries, blackcurrants – together in a bowl with the juice of a squeezed lemon and a little icing sugar to taste. Divide into 12 portions and freeze.

To bring memories of summer to cold winter days, make a delicious summer berry fruit fool. Stir a portion of thawed fruit into 150g of low-fat fromage frais.

Alternatively, heat the berries, and pour them over a dish of icy cold quark, plain low-fat yogurt, or low-fat fromage frais – the contrast between the hot fruit and the icy cold dessert is a delicious taste sensation!

ACTION
RESISTANCE TRAINING

Resistance training is great for improving stamina, strength and co-ordination, and everyone should include some in their activity programme. But what exactly is it?

In a nutshell, resistance training is exercise where your muscles work against some form of resistance. This can be provided by weights, an exercise ball, elastic straps/bands or even your own body weight.

Most people associate resistance training with gyms – all those high-tech machines, and huge free weights to lift. But don't worry if gyms aren't your style, you might prefer to buy a book or video, and gain the benefits of resistance training by using an exercise ball or band, or try an exercise technique such as Pilates (see also page 54), which uses the weight of your own limbs and body to create resistance.

GOING TO THE GYM

Don't be scared of the gym – exercise machines are suitable for almost everyone, even the very weak and the elderly.

Reputable gyms will always insist that you attend an induction session before you're allowed to train on your own. This allows a qualified trainer to gauge the amount that you can safely lift on each machine, and tailor a routine for you, setting you targets to work towards as your fitness increases.

Many people find the social element of going to the gym a great encouragement, particularly if the gym is in a sports centre or leisure complex where there are other facilities, such as a swimming pool and a healthy café.

UNDERSTANDING THE LANGUAGE OF THE GYM

Reps: These are repetitions – the number of times you perform an exercise (such as a bench press) without a break.
Sets: A set is a group of reps, and between each set, you have a rest (see below).
Rests: After your reps, your muscles need a rest. A trainer at your gym will be able to tell you the appropriate rest period for you and your exercises.

Lorna Slater

Lorna, a 49-year-old divorcee, was looking forward to enjoying her flighty fifties. But her eating habits were more like a five-year-old's than a fifty-year-old's, so unless she sorted out her diet it was more likely to be the fatal fifties.

She was a sweet-toothed singleton who snacked constantly on sweets, cakes and chocolate. She ate 27,000 calories a week, which is double the amount recommended.

Her cause was not helped by her desk-bound job. Her sedentary existence meant this five-foot-one and thirteen-and-a-half stone lady was morbidly obese – a third of her body weight was excessive.

Lorna might not have noticed how unhealthy she was becoming, but her workmates did. They secretly nominated her for the series, but luckily Lorna realised she needed to get a grip and rose to the challenge.

And not a moment too soon. Her sugary diet was deficient in fibre and contained nothing fresh. Unsurprisingly, she was lacking in vitamins, especially the vitamins B1 and B2. And her lack of fibre wasn't going to help the discomfort she suffered with her haemorrhoids, as a lack of fibre causes constipation.

A butt-clenching fifty per cent of Brits over the age of fifty have haemorrhoids, or piles. They are varicose veins in the anus and anything that increases abdominal pressure can cause them, including being overweight.

Lorna was desperate to fit back into her favourite dress which she grew out of and used this as her motivation to improve her lifestyle. She struggled initially with the new food and the new way of living and felt quite down, but four weeks in she started to feel so much better physically and therefore became much happier.

CASE STUDY

This five-foot-one and thirteen-and-a-half stone lady was morbidly obese – a third of her body weight was excessive.

MENU PLANNER
JUNE IDEAS

 **JUNE BEST BUYS**

Make the most of:

Cherries
Strawberries
Redcurrants
Gooseberries
Aubergines
Peas
Lettuce
Courgettes
Peppers
Asparagus

Menu 1

Breakfast   Wholegrain roll with nut butter and sliced banana

Lunch   Griddled vegetables with goats' cheese, rosemary and thyme

Dinner   Steamed chicken with broccoli, vine tomatoes and sweet potato mash

Zingy fresh fruit salad

Menu 2

Breakfast   Dried fruit compote

Lunch   Mixed vegetable, goats' cheese and rice salad

Dinner   Classic steak burgers with griddled tomatoes

Fruit crumble yogurt

Menu 1

☼ Wholegrain roll with nut butter and sliced banana

1 Cut the rolls in half and spread with nut butter.
2 Chop the banana into circles and top each half of the rolls with them.

TIP
● Try this with the rolls lightly crisped under the grill before you spread them with nut butter – delicious!

4 wholegrain rolls

Nut butter (peanut, almond or cashew) for spreading

2 large bananas, sliced

Serves 4

☀ Griddled vegetables with goat's cheese, rosemary and thyme

1 Preheat a ridged griddle pan or an electric health grill. Place all the vegetables in a large bowl with the olive oil and chopped herbs. Season with black pepper and toss together.
2 Place the vegetables on the griddle or grill (close the lid if you're using an electric health grill). Cook for 6–8 minutes until tender and lightly browned, turning occasionally if using a griddle.
3 Arrange the rocket leaves on 4 plates. Top with piles of the grilled vegetables. Grill or griddle the tomatoes for 1–2 minutes until just softened and lightly browned. Place on top of the grilled peppers, courgette and onion.
4 Sprinkle the vegetables with the goats' cheese and pine nuts, if using, top with the basil leaves and drizzle with a little balsamic vinegar. Serve warm.

> **Health fact:** Carrots are super-rich in betacarotene, which the body converts to vitamin A – important for healthy eyes, skin and a strong immune system. Eating a diet rich in betacarotene helps protect against certain types of cancer.

1 yellow pepper, deseeded and quartered

1 red pepper, deseeded and quartered

1 large courgette, trimmed and diagonally sliced

1 small red onion, peeled and cut into wedges

80g goats' cheese, crumbled

1tbsp virgin olive oil

2tsp chopped fresh rosemary

2tsp chopped fresh thyme

Small bag rocket leaves

2 large vine tomatoes, sliced

Small handful fresh basil leaves

25g pine nuts (optional)

Freshly ground black pepper

Balsamic vinegar, to serve

Serves 4 as a light lunch or supper

☾ Steamed chicken with broccoli, vine tomatoes and sweet potato mash

800g sweet potatoes, peeled and cut into 4cm pieces

4 boneless chicken breasts (preferably free range or organic), each about 175g, skinned

3–5 sprigs fresh thyme (preferably lemon thyme), chopped

4 stalks cherry vine tomatoes, each holding around 7 tomatoes

12 tender-stem broccoli stalks, trimmed and cut in half lengthways

15g butter or a little skimmed milk

Freshly ground black pepper

Fresh thyme sprigs, to garnish (optional)

Serves 4

1 Boil the sweet potato until tender.
2 Tip the potatoes into a bowl and mash with the butter or milk and ground black pepper to taste.
3 Fill a steamer with water and place the chicken in a steamer basket. Sprinkle the chicken with thyme leaves and season with freshly ground black pepper and steam for about 20 minutes until the chicken is completely cooked and no pinkness remains in the centre. Keep warm.
4 Refill the steamer with water and place the tomatoes and broccoli in the basket. Steam until the vegetables are tender.
5 Spoon the sweet potato mash onto warmed plates and top with the chicken.
6 Serve with the broccoli and tomatoes, garnished with fresh thyme, if liked.

> **Health fact:** Broccoli contains compounds called isothiocyanates, which could help protect us from certain cancers, including lung cancer.

Zingy fresh fruit salad

4 clementines or mandarins, halved

2 oranges, peeled and segmented

1 apple, quartered, cored and sliced

1 pear, quartered, cored and sliced

1 small bunch seedless grapes, halved

2 small bananas, sliced

Serves 4

1 Juice the clementines or mandarins using the citrus press and pour into a large serving bowl. Add the orange segments, apple, pear, grapes and bananas. Toss gently together and serve.

> **Health fact:** Bananas are a good source of potassium and a type of fibre which encourages the growth of 'friendly' bacteria in the gut. Apples are a good source of pectin – a type of soluble fibre that can help reduce high blood-cholesterol levels. Oranges are an excellent source of vitamin C.

Menu 2
☀ Dried fruit compote

1 Carefully remove the zest from half the orange in wide strips using a knife – avoid the bitter pith. Place in a medium saucepan. Cut the orange in half and extract the juice from both halves. Pour the orange juice into the saucepan with the zest. Add the apple juice, mixed dried fruits and cinnamon.

2 Cook over a low heat for 10 minutes. Allow the juice to bubble gently and stir occasionally until the fruit is plump and tender. Remove from the heat and set aside for 5 minutes. Remove the cinnamon stick and serve the compote warm or cold with spoonfuls of yogurt and a sprinkling of roughly chopped nuts and seeds if liked.

Health fact: Dried apricots are a reasonable non-meat source of iron, which is needed to prevent anaemia. They are also a good source of betacarotene, which can be converted to vitamin A in the body.

1 large orange, well washed

200ml pressed apple juice

350g mixed 'ready to eat' dried fruits, such as apples, peaches, apricots, pears and prunes, cut in half if large

½ a cinnamon stick

Fat-free bio-yogurt and roughly chopped nuts and seeds, to serve

Serves 4

Just cooking for one or two? Why not cool the compote then transfer to a bowl, cover and keep in the fridge for up to 2 days.

Mixed vegetable, goats' cheese and rice salad

100g brown rice

2tsp olive oil

1 red and 1 yellow pepper, deseeded and cut into 3cm pieces

1 medium leek, trimmed and sliced

150g green beans, trimmed

1 head broccoli, cut into small florets

125g frozen peas

80g soft, mild goats' cheese

Freshly ground black pepper

Serves 4

1 Bring 600ml cold water to the boil in a saucepan and add the rice. Return to the boil and cook for 25–35 minutes until tender, adding more water if necessary. Tip into a sieve and rinse under running water until cold. Drain well and transfer to a large serving bowl.

2 While the rice is cooking, heat the oil in a large frying pan over a gentle heat and cook the pepper and leek for 5 minutes until softened and very lightly browned, stirring regularly. Set aside to cool.

3 Bring a medium pan of water to the boil, add the beans and return to the boil. Cook for 2 minutes. Add the broccoli and peas. Return water to the boil, then drain at once. Rinse the vegetables in a colander under running water until cold.

4 Toss all the vegetables with the cooked rice and season with ground black pepper. Spoon onto plates and top with crumbled goats' cheese. Serve with a large mixed-leaf salad.

TIP

● This salad is also great served cold in packed lunches.

Wholegrain (brown) rice provides fibre, magnesium, phosphorus, vitamin B1 and iron. It's also a good source of folic acid, which is vital during pregnancy, as well as helping protect the heart.

Lean red meat is an excellent source of protein and iron. Low iron stores can cause lethargy, fatigue and difficulty in concentrating.

☾ Classic steak burgers with griddled tomatoes

1 Place the mince, onion, garlic and herbs in a large bowl. Season with ground black pepper and mix with a spoon until well combined. Lightly oil a griddle or electric health grill and preheat.

2 Form the mince mixture into four balls and flatten into burger shapes. Place on the griddle or grill (and close the lid if using a grill) and cook for 5–7 minutes or until completely cooked and no pinkness remains.

3 Cut each tomato stalk in half to make four mini-vines, each holding 5–6 cherry tomatoes. Add the tomatoes to the griddle for the last 2 minutes of cooking time. Mix the yogurt and horseradish sauce, or mustard, in a small bowl.

4 Serve the burgers topped with the horseradish cream and accompanied by the grilled tomatoes and seasonal vegetables or a large mixed salad.

500g pack very lean minced steak (not more than 5% fat)

1 small onion, peeled and finely chopped (about 100g prepared weight)

1 garlic clove, peeled and crushed

1tsp mixed dried herbs

2 stalks of vine cherry tomatoes

Freshly ground black pepper

Sunflower oil, for greasing

For the horseradish cream:

4tbsp fat-free bio-yogurt

1tsp hot horseradish sauce (or, as an alternative, wholegrain mustard)

Serves 4

Fruit crumble yogurt

1 Preheat the oven to 200°C/Gas 6. Lightly oil a nonstick baking tray. Put the oats in a bowl and stir in the apple juice and 1tsp of the sugar. Stand for 5 minutes, stirring occasionally.

2 Tip onto the baking tray and spread evenly with a wooden spoon. Bake for about 10 minutes until golden, stirring halfway through the cooking time. Remove from the oven and leave to cool.

3 Roughly chop half the strawberries and set aside. Blend the remainder with the yogurt and remaining sugar using a stick blender (or in a food processor) until smooth. Stir in the reserved chopped strawberries and spoon into 4 dishes. Sprinkle with the oat crumble and serve.

¼ tsp sunflower oil, for greasing

50g porridge oats

2tbsp pressed apple juice

1½ tsp unrefined light brown muscovado sugar

250g fresh strawberries

2 x 150g pots 0%-fat Greek yogurt

Serves 4

july

FOOD, MOOD AND HORMONES

How we feel affects what we eat – it's so much harder to resist temptation when we're feeling low. And we all have our comfort foods – the little helpers we turn to in order to boost our moods.

New habits

It's time to change your mood-boosters. Here are some tips to get you started.

- If you always have a cappuccino and chocolate muffin when you go out with a friend, have a decaffeinated coffee instead, with a lower sugar treat, such as a scone.
- If you always have a couple of chocolate biscuits with your cup of tea, cut it down to one. Have plain biscuits or – even better – oatcakes.
- Gradually wean yourself off the sugar in your tea or coffee.

Remember, it can take time to create a new habit, but the benefits are worth it.

MOOD AND FOOD

Our mood can often dictate the food we eat. We may reach for a cup of coffee to get us moving in the morning, or dive into a tub of ice cream after a particularly rotten day at work.

And in return, food certainly affects our mood. For example, that cup of coffee is a powerful stimulant – it perks us up. And the ice cream boosts our blood sugar, making us feel better (albeit briefly, until all too quickly, our blood-sugar levels fall again). But the effect isn't just in our bodies – it's in our minds, too.

We form very strong psychological associations with foods, especially our comfort foods. In our minds, coffee may be entwined with having a cappuccino with friends, and ice cream with happy childhood memories and being given ice cream as a treat. If a food you enjoy is used as a reward, it's very likely that your brain will file it away as a 'feel-good food', and whenever you eat it, you'll feel better.

The problem is, a lot of our 'foody props' are high in fat and sugar, rather than the nutrients we should be feeding our bodies if we want to be kind to them. A quick stimulant hit from caffeine or sugar leaves us feeling great for a while, but sadly the sensation soon passes. Add to that the guilt associated with giving in to temptation, and the feeling isn't a good one.

So, what's the solution? Once again, it's back to blood-sugar levels. As our blood-sugar levels fall, we can begin to feel anxious and twitchy – an attack of the munchies sets in and we reach for the sugary snack we 'know' will make us feel better. Our blood-sugar level quickly rises, but soon falls again, leaving us in the same state as before. Unless we are suffering from diabetes, our bodies are able to maintain our blood-sugar levels between a safe minimum and maximum – when they rise too high, we produce insulin which removes the sugar from the bloodstream and stores it away. But if we keep our blood-sugar levels cruising along on an even keel, we can avoid all those unpleasant feelings caused by our levels rising and falling like a roller coaster.

So, how do we keep our blood-sugar levels stable? The secret is those 'slow burn', low-GI, low-GL foods we introduced in April's chapter.

By reaching for a wholemeal bagel with low-fat cream cheese and a slick of honey, instead of a slice of cake, you'll get that sweet, indulgent taste, but the whole grains and the protein in the cheese will give your energy levels a slow, sustained boost.

MOOD STABILISING FOODS – ON THE MOVE

When we're out and about, it's often hard to stick to regular meal times, which can play havoc with our blood-sugar levels. When we're on the move and need to grab a quick bite to eat, we may not be able to select the kind of virtuous foods we'd choose at home. But try to avoid anything that's high in sugar and instead go for slow-fuel options, such as a baked potato with a protein-rich filling such as baked beans, or a low-sugar oat flapjack.

Be prepared! Before you go out, pack some 'slow burn' treats, to tide you and your mood over and boost your energy, so you don't reach for a sugary snack instead. Before your stomach begins to rumble and you get that jittery, craving feeling, grab one of these snacks:

- Nuts (unsalted) and raisins, or trail mix. The fibre in the dried fruit and the protein in the nuts make this a 'slow fuel' snack.
- Dried figs or apricots.
- Seeds, such as pumpkin seeds or sunflower seeds.
- Oatcakes.
- Plain popcorn (avoid those that are laden with butter, sugar or salt).
- Sticks of raw vegetables – try carrot, celery, peppers or cucumber (remove the seeds and watery core).

Enemies of calm moods and stable blood-sugar levels include:

- Skipping meals
- Alcohol
- Caffeine
- Cigarettes

CAVEMAN TASTES

Our bodies evolved to crave sugary and fatty foods. When life was harsh and food hard to come by, it made sense to seek out and gobble down high-energy foods – a fatty haunch of meat, or a chunk of sweetly dripping honeycomb. Putting on weight helped us to survive the lean times when food was scarce.

The problem is, nowadays we're surrounded by sweet, fatty convenience foods. Our brains our hard-wired to 'want' them, the marketing people tempt us to buy them – but they're not what our bodies want or need at all.

FEEL-GOOD FISH

While slow-fuel foods and stable blood-sugar levels help keep your mood steady, eating enough fish could help prevent depression!

Population studies have found that countries where the population eats a lot of oily fish – the number one source of omega-3 essential fatty acids – have particularly low rates of depression. And medical trials of omega-3s have shown encouraging results in improving people's depression symptoms.

It certainly looks as though omega-3s are involved in good moods, so it makes sense to boost your intake of these beneficial fats, found mainly in oily fish, but also in flaxseeds and flaxseed oil.

Non-food mood boosters

Why not give yourself a treat that doesn't involve food:

- Go window-shopping
- Stroke a dog or cuddle a cat
- Phone a friend
- Curl up with a good book
- Watch a movie
- Treat yourself to a haircut or manicure
- Go for a walk

The chromium connection

Studies suggest that making sure we get enough of the mineral chromium in our diets could help balance our blood-sugar levels.

Good chromium containing foods include:

- Red meat
- Wholegrain cereals
- Nuts
- Beans, such as red kidney beans, mung beans and aduki beans
- Brewer's yeast

Scientists have found that 'dummy pills' can sometimes make a person feel better, as they 'expect' the tablets to make them well (this is called the placebo effect). In a similar way, a person may feel buzzy and wired after drinking decaffeinated coffee if he or she thinks that it's a regular, caffeinated cup.

Oily fish – brain food

Omega-3 fatty acids:
- May help fight depression.
- Are involved in the development of the brain, while the embryo is still in the womb. In a study supervised by doctors, the babies of mothers who took an omega-3 supplement during pregnancy scored higher in 'baby IQ tests'. If you are pregnant and want to take supplements please consult your doctor first.
- Population studies have found that people in countries with a diet high in oily fish tend to suffer less from dementia in old age.
- Children with ADHD (attention deficit hyperactivity disorder) have been found to have lower levels of omega-3s in their bodies, and exciting evidence is emerging that supplementing their diets with omega-3s can help control their condition.

ESSENTIAL OMEGAS

The omega fatty acids are a group of polyunsaturated fats with an amazing range of health benefits – and not just for your mind.

Omega-3 fatty acids

These beneficial fats are good for your cholesterol score – they lower the level of 'bad' LDL cholesterol in the blood, reducing your risk of cardiovascular disease (heart disease and stroke). There is also a 'good' kind of cholesterol (called HDL) that helps prevent cardiovascular disease, and omega-3s raise the level of this. They also help lower your blood pressure.

These fantastic fats also have an anti-inflammatory effect, and scientific studies suggest that they may be helpful in treating and preventing inflammatory diseases such as rheumatoid arthritis, Crohn's disease and ulcerative colitis.

The best sources of Omega-3s are fish, such as mackerel, salmon, sardines and herring. Canned oily fish is a good source, except for tuna, as the omega-3s in tuna are lost during the canning process.

Omega-3s are also found in flaxseeds (linseeds) but the omega-3s from this vegetarian source are less easy for the body to use. For optimum health, we should eat four portions of oily fish each week (though pregnant women should limit this to two).

Omega-6 fatty acids

These beneficial fats have similar health effects to omega-3s, though omega-3s have slightly greater health benefits. Exciting new research has also shown promising results for omega-6s improving skin conditions such as eczema, and in helping to reduce the risk of type-2 diabetes.

Omega-6s are found in nuts and seeds, as well as some vegetable oils – corn oil, sunflower oil and safflower oil.

Fats in balance

The balance of omega-3 versus omega-6 fatty acids is important, since they 'compete' in the body. If you have too much omega-6 in comparison to omega-3, this cancels out some of the health benefits.

Most of us find it easier to get enough of the omega-6 fatty acids, since they're found in commonly eaten foods such as eggs, poultry, sunflower oil and fat spreads. It's the omega-3s we need to work harder at, concentrating on those oily fish, and flaxseeds and their oil. You can also boost your input by eating omega-3 enriched eggs.

There's no need to get hung up about getting your ratio right – the best way to come close to achieving it is just to make an extra effort to increase the omega-3s in your diet.

Good foods to boos your mood:

◆ Chicken
◆ Turkey
◆ Tuna
◆ Salmon
◆ Kidney beans
◆ Oats (below)
◆ Lentils

FOOD, MOLECULES AND THE BRAIN

Scientists are discovering that the food we eat can affect the chemical messengers in our brain, called neurotransmitters, which influence the way we think and feel. Although we don't yet fully understand the links between our diets and the neurotransmitters, it appears that certain foods can alter the levels of these brain chemicals, helping us to stay calm and contented. Antidepressants like Prozac work by increasing the available levels of a neurotransmitter in the brain. Could foods have a similar mood-boosting effect? It's certainly a possibility.

There's a brain chemical called serotonin that enhances our mood and helps us to sleep. It's also involved in the feeling of fullness after eating. In order to make serotonin, the brain needs an amino acid (a protein building block) called tryptophan, and it's possible that by eating foods containing tryptophan we can help our brains to make more of that mood-enhancing serotonin.

SOMETIMES IT'S HARD TO BE A WOMAN . . .
Premenstrual Syndrome

Once a month, PMS makes many women's lives a misery.

But saying 'it's just hormones' is too simplistic an answer. Nutrition plays a role as well, as does stress:

Blood-sugar levels

Women who feel that they're particularly sensitive to the anxious, jittery feeling that wobbly blood-sugar levels give them often say that this becomes worse in the days before their period. They also tend to find that taking steps to even out their blood-sugar levels helps significantly. Once more they need to choose those 'slow burn' foods – complex carbohydrates (starchy foods), concentrating on wholemeal and brown foods, with moderate amounts of low-fat protein.

Helpful nutrients

Magnesium – As many as eighty per cent of women suffering from PMS have been found to have low magnesium levels. Although it isn't possible to say that the lack of magnesium is definitely contributing to their symptoms, taking especial care that you're getting enough of this important mineral has to be a good idea. Good sources of magnesium include whole grains, beans and lentils, green leafy vegetables and tofu.

Essential fatty acids – Many women find that taking a supplement containing essential fatty acids, such as evening primrose oil, starflower oil, or fish oil, helps their premenstrual symptoms. Yet another beneficial effect from our friends the omega-3 and omega-6 fatty acids, and all the more reason to enjoy as many foods rich in them, such as oily fish, nuts and seeds, as possible!

Food and the menopause

As with PMS, poor nutrition and stress can intensify menopause symptoms. If you're prone to feeling low, pay particular attention to the advice on mood-balancing earlier in this chapter. And try to give your body as nutritious a diet as possible, to help it cope with the hormonal shifts you're experiencing.

You should also eat foods rich in calcium and vitamin D, to keep up your bone strength – low-fat dairy products, tinned fish with edible bones (such as salmon and sardines), and tofu are good sources. Many low-fat spreads are enriched with vitamin D, but the main source of vitamin D in this country is sunlight. Exposing the skin to sunlight sets in motion a reaction that makes vitamin D in the body, so try to get outside for at least a few minutes each day.

Antioxidant-rich foods such as fruit, vegetables, nuts and seeds also help protect against heart disease and stroke.

What about soya protein?

Japanese women, who eat a lot of soya foods, suffer less from menopausal symptoms such as hot flushes, than Western women. It's thought that the phyto-oestrogens (plant oestrogens) in the soya could be helping their symptoms, and many women swear by a soya-rich diet to ease them through the menopause. Others take dietary supplements of the individual phyto-chemicals, such as the soya isoflavones daidzein and genistein.

Soya protein is also an excellent low-fat protein source, and probably helps promote heart health by reducing levels of the 'bad' LDL form of cholesterol. However, the scientific evidence on the effectiveness and safety of isoflavone supplements in the form of tablets or capsules is conflicting, and more research is needed before all women are advised to take them. Increasing the amount of soya protein you eat is a much better way of increasing these natural chemicals in your body.

Foods containing soya protein include:

- Tofu
- Tempeh
- Soya beans
- Soya mince
- Soya burgers
- Soya milk (choose a calcium-enriched variety)

ACTION
LOOK AFTER YOUR MIND

Your mind needs looking after as well as your body. Exercising the brain gives you a real sense of achievement and feeling of wellbeing, but don't worry – it isn't strenuous!

Stimulate the mind

Relax with a good book (maybe try one of those classics you promised yourself you'd read one day), listen to a piece of classical music, do a crossword, a trivia quiz or, if you're a numbers fan, try your hand at Kakuro. Or make time to visit a museum or an art gallery. If you like to meet other people, you could join a debating society, an investment society or a book-reading group. If there isn't an established group near you, why not start one with a group of friends or work colleagues?

Make time to have fun

Countless studies have found that having a really good laugh with a few friends or members of the family can lower blood pressure, trigger the release of the feel-good chemicals called endorphins, and reduce the old enemy, stress.

Make time to meditate

Just five minutes of simple meditation will make you feel relaxed and revitalised. Find a quiet room. Sit comfortably with your eyes closed and your arms and legs relaxed. Take about twenty deep slow breaths while you try to empty your mind and listen to the rhythm of your breathing. Then slowly open your eyes and sit quietly for about a minute. For more on meditation, see page 183 in November's chapter.

Set yourself goals

Set yourself goals – it helps you feel more in control of your life. Make sure your targets are realistic, and set goals with different timescales, for example phoning a friend tonight, fixing that wobbly shelf this week, and brushing up on your holiday French by this time next year.

Celebrate your successes

Don't wait for mountainous achievements before celebrating – enjoy your successes, however small. Spend a few minutes each day thinking of the things that went well and give yourself a pat on the back. Try not to concentrate on what you thought were mistakes – the chances are no one else even noticed them – and don't worry about tomorrow. Remember the old song, 'Accentuate the positive, Eliminate the negative' – it's a great maxim for a healthy mind.

Allyson Connor and Angela Goodall

Allyson Connor, 23, and her mother, Angela Goodall, 51, lived together in Staffordshire. They were a great duo with a very close relationship, but they tipped the scales at 21½ stone each, and were both not only big eaters, but big drinkers too.

Between them Allyson and Angela could get through 13½ litres of alcohol in a week, adding up to 10,000 calories or the food equivalent of 80 doughnuts.

As Allyson was a barmaid in her local pub she often ate late at night, usually junk food or a fry-up that Angela had waiting for her when she got home. On nights out she might binge-drink up to ten pints. Her favourite hangover cure was oatcakes with greasy fillings, and to make matters worse, she also had a weakness for pork scratchings.

Angela would often enjoy two or three large vodkas in an evening and found that she always had diarrhoea the morning after she had a drink.

Allyson and Angela were in desperate need of Gillian's help to break the vicious cycle of binge drinking and eating. Gillian confronted them with Allyson's bad-food table of everything she had consumed in a week. As well as numerous fry-ups and beef-and-onion pies, it featured several bags of pork scratchings and sixteen and a half pints of lager. Allyson cried and told Gillian that she was ashamed of herself. Having dealt with the terrible extent of their eating habits, Gillian knew she also had to make Allyson and Angela face the facts about their binge drinking, so she showed them the food equivalent of the amount of alcohol they drank in a week - 135 fatty rashers of bacon.

Having consulted their GP, it was time for Allyson and Angela to become acquainted with their new diet. Gillian devised an eight-week food plan designed to flush out toxins and replenish their depleted stocks of vitamins and minerals. Fast foods were out and fresh foods were in. They used to start their days with a hangover; now they were to start it with sage tea. Gillian replaced their hangover cures with smoked tofu and rice burgers, hoping the tofu would prevent them missing the bacon they were so used to.

Two weeks into the diet, Angela and Allyson were missing the huge amount of meat they used to eat, and struggling with some of the foods such as sushi rolls and avocado. Meanwhile, Angela's liver-function tests showed raised scores, indicating damage. It was not too late to repair the damage however, and under Gillian's guidance both women were finding it easy to turn their back on the booze. They were even beginning to enjoy the food.

Gillian also introduced Angela and Allyson to some gentle exercise. For Angela, it was swimming, and for Allyson, boxercise, which is great for burning calories and toning muscles.

Eight weeks on, and it was another great result for Gillian. She returned to find that Angela had lost nearly three stone and Allyson has dropped four dress sizes. Both were brimming with energy and confidence. Neither were missing alcohol and they had both finally realised that their old diet was stopping them feeling and looking well.

MENU PLANNER
JULY IDEAS

 **JULY BEST BUYS**

Make the most of:
Red and white currants
Raspberries
Strawberries
Gooseberries
Salad vegetables
Broccoli
French beans
Courgettes
Peas and mangetout
Marrows

Menu 1

Breakfast   Summer berry breakfast

Lunch   Baked mushrooms with Dolcelatte

Dinner   Lemon and dill salmon with steamed vegetables

Vanilla custards with berry fruits

Menu 2

Breakfast   Scrambled eggs with grilled tomatoes

Lunch   Tofu vegetable noodle soup

Dinner   Garlic and herb chicken

Orange and mango frozen dessert

Menu 1
☼ Summer berry breakfast

300g summer berries (raspberries, blackberries, blackcurrants)

2 x 150g cartons low-fat natural yogurt

300ml apple juice

2tbsp toasted sunflower seeds

1tsp honey, if needed

Serves 4

1. Put the fruit, yogurt and apple juice into a liquidiser and blend until smooth.
2. Pour into 4 tall glasses and sprinkle with toasted sunflower seeds. Serve immediately.

Health fact: The crunchy sunflower seeds are a good source of the omega-6 essential fatty acids which promote healthy skin and could even help prevent type-2 diabetes.

☼ Baked mushrooms with Dolcelatte

2 slices medium wholegrain bread, toasted

2 spring onions, trimmed and roughly chopped

3tbsp roughly chopped parsley

30g walnut halves

4 large field or portabella mushrooms, each about 50g

40g Dolcelatte cheese

Freshly ground black pepper

A large, lightly dressed salad, to serve

Serves 4

1. Preheat the oven to 200°C/Gas 6.
2. Break each slice of bread into 4 or 5 pieces and place in a food processor with the onion, parsley and walnuts. Blend for a few seconds until the mixture is very finely chopped. Season with ground black pepper.
3. Peel away the skin from the mushrooms and discard. Remove the stalks. Place the mushrooms upside down on a baking tray lined with nonstick foil. Divide the herb stuffing amongst the mushrooms and press down lightly with fingertips.
4. Top with small pieces of the cheese and bake for 10 minutes until the cheese has melted and the mushrooms are tender. Serve hot with a large, lightly dressed salad.

Health fact: The cheese contains calcium, which helps protect against osteoporosis and may also help control blood pressure. Eat full-fat cheese in small amounts, as it is high in saturated fat.

☾ Lemon and dill salmon

1 Fill the bottom of a steamer with cold water. Toss the potatoes with the oil and parsley and place in a steamer basket. Steam until the potatoes are tender. Transfer to a serving dish and keep warm.
2 Place the salmon fillets in a lightly oiled ovenproof plate. Squeeze the lemon juice over the salmon fillets, top with the lemon slices and sprinkle with dill. Season with a little ground black pepper. Place the plate in a steamer and arrange the mixed vegetables around the plate. Steam for about 18–20 minutes until the vegetables are tender and the fish is cooked. Serve with extra lemon wedges for squeezing.

> **Health fact:** Salmon is an excellent source of the essential omega-3 fatty acids, and all of the fresh vegetables are brimming with vitamin C, which is a powerful antioxidant that protects cells from free-radical damage and boosts immunity.

400g baby new potatoes, halved

2tsp olive oil

2tbsp chopped fresh parsley

2tbsp freshly squeezed lemon juice

4 fresh salmon fillets, each about 150g skinned

8 thin slices of lemon

2tbsp chopped fresh dill

200g baby carrots, trimmed and cut in half lengthways (if thick)

200g baby corn, trimmed (or green beans)

200g sugar snap peas, trimmed

Freshly ground black pepper

Lemon wedges, for squeezing

Serves 4

Vanilla custards with berry fruits

1 Fill the bottom of a steamer with cold water.
2 Put 4 very lightly oiled 150ml ramekin dishes into the steamer basket. Beat the eggs in a medium bowl until smooth.
3 Blend 2tbsp of the milk with the cornflour and set aside. Pour the remaining milk into a saucepan, add the sugar and heat gently for 2–3 minutes until hot, stirring occasionally. Do not allow to boil.
4 Remove the milk from the hob and whisk into the eggs. Stir in the cornflour mixture and vanilla. Transfer to a jug then carefully pour into the ramekin dishes. Cover each dish loosely with a piece of foil.
5 Put the lid on the steamer and steam for 20 minutes until the egg mixture is lightly set. Remove the lid, turn the steamer off and allow the custards to cool for 20 minutes. Place custards in the fridge and chill for at least 2 hours before serving.
6 Loosen the sides of each custard with a round-bladed knife and turn out onto dessert plates. Serve with lots of fresh berries and decorate with fresh mint leaves.

3 medium free-range eggs

450ml skimmed milk

1tbsp cornflour

2tbsp light brown muscovado sugar

½ tsp vanilla extract or a few drops of vanilla essence

Sunflower oil, for greasing

Mint leaves and fresh strawberries, raspberries and blueberries, to serve

Serves 4

Menu 2

☀ Scrambled eggs with tomatoes

4 large, ripe vine tomatoes, halved

6 large free-range eggs

3tbsp skimmed milk

4 medium slices wholegrain bread

Freshly ground black pepper

Serves 4

1 Place the tomatoes on a grill pan and season with freshly ground black pepper. Cook under a preheated hot grill for 4–5 minutes until cooked.

2 In a bowl whisk the eggs with the milk, then season with black pepper.

3 Put the eggs and milk mixture into a nonstick saucepan and cook gently for 2–3 minutes. Stir with a wooden spoon every now and then until the eggs are just set – try not to stir too much or overcook the eggs as they could become dry. Toast the bread.

4 Divide the toast between 4 plates. Top with the scrambled eggs and finish with the hot, grilled tomatoes.

☼ Tofu vegetable noodle soup

100g wholewheat spaghetti, broken in half, or thin egg noodles

2cm piece fresh root ginger, peeled and cut into thin shreds

1 garlic clove, peeled and sliced

600ml cold water

1tsp organic vegetable bouillon (stock) powder

2tsp organic wheat-free tamari soy sauce

3 spring onions, trimmed and sliced

½ a small red pepper, deseeded and sliced

85g broccoli, cut into small florets

85g mangetout, trimmed and halved

6 baby corn, trimmed and sliced into 2cm lengths

250g fresh tofu, drained and cut into 1.5cm cubes

1tbsp chopped fresh coriander (optional)

Serves 4

1 Cook the spaghetti or noodles until tender according to the pack instructions. Drain in a sieve under running water until cold. Set aside.

2 Place the ginger, garlic, water, stock powder and soy sauce in a large saucepan and bring to the boil. Add the spring onions, red pepper, broccoli, mangetout and baby corn.

3 Return to the boil and cook for 2 minutes. Stir in the spaghetti or noodles and then gently add the tofu, ensuring that it is completely immersed in the cooking liquor.

4 Heat through gently for 2 minutes without stirring until the tofu is heated through. Ladle into bowls and serve immediately, sprinkled with fresh coriander if liked.

> **Health fact:** Tofu is made from soya bean curd and is rich in hormone-like compounds called phyto-oestrogens (plant oestrogens), which may help reduce the risk of hormone-related cancers and reduce the symptoms of the menopause.

TIP

- For a more fiery flavour, add half a finely chopped red chilli to the garlic, ginger, water, stock and soy sauce in step 2.

☾ Garlic and herb chicken

1 Cut the chicken breast carefully horizontally almost all the way through the middle with a knife and open out. Place in a shallow dish and add the olive oil, lemon juice, parsley and garlic. Season with a little ground black pepper. Cover and leave to marinate in the fridge for 30 minutes.
2 Lightly oil and preheat an electric health grill or ridged griddle pan. Lift the chicken out of the marinade with a fork and shake off any excess. Grill for 3–5 minutes.
3 Turn the chicken over, close and grill for a further 2–3 minutes until the chicken is thoroughly cooked through and no pinkness remains.
4 Remove from the grill and stand for 3 minutes.
5 Serve with a small jacket potato and a large mixed salad or freshly cooked seasonal vegetables.

4 boneless chicken breasts, preferably free range or organic, skinned

1tbsp olive oil, plus extra for greasing

Freshly squeezed juice of a lemon

4tbsp chopped fresh parsley

1 garlic clove, peeled and crushed

Freshly ground black pepper

Large mixed salad or seasonal vegetables, to serve

Serves 4

> **Health fact:** Garlic is a heart-healthy food – it can help reduce high blood pressure and high blood-cholesterol levels.

Orange and mango frozen dessert

1 Stand the mango on a chopping board and carefully cut either side of the large, flat stone using a sharp knife. Scoop out the flesh with a dessertspoon and place in a food processor or blender. Add the bananas and orange juice.
2 Blend on low for a few seconds, then switch to high and blend until smooth. Transfer to a rigid freezer-proof container. Freeze for 3 hours, then remove and stir well with a fork to break up the ice crystals. Return to the freezer for a further 2 hours, then remove and stir once more. Freeze until solid.
3 Stand at room temperature for 10–15 minutes to soften before serving. Spoon into dessert dishes and decorate with fresh raspberries and mint leaves.

1 large ripe mango

2 bananas, peeled and thickly sliced

150ml fresh orange juice

Fresh raspberries and mint leaves, to decorate

Serves 4

> **Health fact:** Mangoes are an excellent source of the antioxidant vitamins A, C and E, which help support the immune system.

august

HEALTHY EATING – OUT AND ABOUT

Relax and enjoy eating away from home. Just think what a treat it is to eat a meal which you haven't had to shop for, prepare and cook! And you can still eat healthily when someone else is wielding the wooden spoon and doing the cooking.

- Eat breakfast – a healthy one every day
- Get the hydration habit – drink plenty of water

Whether it's eating in the work canteen, on holiday or in a restaurant, all you need to do to make healthy choices is study the menu and work out what is likely to be in the dishes and their method of cooking. Then ask your server or waiter anything you're not sure about, and confidently choose a healthy dish to enjoy.

HOW TO HANDLE HOLIDAYS

Healthy good intentions don't have to go out of the window when you go on holiday. So long as you make sensible choices and don't throw caution to the wind, you can eat in hotels and restaurants, without undoing all the good you have done at home.

Every country has its healthy options; it's just a matter of finding them. And one of the wonderful things about many foreign holiday destinations is that you'll often discover local food stalls and markets in even the smallest towns and villages selling fantastic fruit – the perfect anytime snack – and restaurants serving fish straight from the sea. Could there be anything nicer than eating peaches that were on the tree a few hours earlier or grilled fish cooked in front of you, as you sip a long cool glass of freshly pressed fruit juice, at a beachside barbecue restaurant?

Make the most of the opportunity to savour new flavours, try new dishes, and sample exotic fruit and vegetables. Aim to come home with a clutch of new recipes to add to your healthy eating repertoire and perhaps even a jar or two of local specialities to spice up your cooking at home.

Even if you're not the most adventurous when it comes to food you'll find that international cuisine is available in most countries – and not only the pizza, chips and burgers variety – so you should always be able to find some familiar healthy dishes.

When you're eating out, be aware of dishes that are likely to be high in fat or sugar, find restaurants where food is cooked to order (even if you have to wait a little longer for your meal to arrive) and don't be afraid to ask if you are not sure about the way a dish is cooked and what it contains.

SELF-CATERING

The secret of self-catering holidays is to keep meals simple. You don't want to be stuck in the kitchen preparing a cordon bleu delight while everyone else is enjoying themselves.

Enlist the help of the family in preparing meals; even children enjoy the novelty of preparing meals on holiday. Or if you're away with your friends then resist the urge to throw a pizza in the oven and instead take advantage of local foods. Look around for farm shops and markets where you can buy locally grown produce and fresh meat, fish and poultry.

If the weather is good then eat meals outside in the shade when you can. Somehow eating outside seems more relaxing and also gives you the opportunity for a good chat.

If you're holidaying overseas, always follow the food safety advice regarding whether it is safe to drink tap water, have ice in drinks or eat salads etc.

> If you are self-catering, decant a few of your favourite herbs and spices into tiny plastic bags before you go, to add flavour to simple dishes. They won't take up much space.

TURN UP THE HEAT

Summer is a great time for barbecues – so make the most of them. A simple piece of marinated meat, chicken or fish with an enormous salad and some chunks of crusty wholemeal bread makes the perfect alfresco meal for all the family.

Tip: Always ensure that barbecued meat (especially chicken) is thoroughly cooked, right the way through. But don't let your barbecued meat char or burn as this can produce chemicals linked with an increased risk of cancer.

TAKEAWAYS

There's no getting away from it – takeaway food is popular. As a nation we spend a staggering £1.4 billion a year on carry-out food. Unfortunately, most takeaway food is horrendously high in saturated fat and salt, and correspondingly low in fibre, vitamins and minerals.

If you do want the occasional takeaway, here are some top tips to help you make the more healthy choices.

INDIAN:

The 'baddies':

- Dishes with cream (tikka masala, korma, passanda). Look out for words like 'rich', or 'creamy' on the menu and avoid these dishes.
- Anything deep-fried or high in fat (bhajis, samosa, pakora, pilau rice, naan bread, poppadums). Naan breads are a real fat trap, and can be heavy on sugar – fruity peshawari naan has lots of added sugar and coconut.

Healthier alternatives:

- Dishes cooked in the tandoor oven – these are the lowest fat option you'll find. Go for tandoori chicken or tandoori king prawns, or chicken or lamb tikka, served with salad. You could opt for a starter-sized portion of a tandoori or tikka dish with a double-sized salad. But beware tikka masala dishes as they come with a high-fat sauce.
- Curries with tomato-based sauces.
- Plain boiled rice.
- Chapattis.

CHINESE:

The 'baddies':

- Anything deep-fried or battered, such as prawn toasts, fried rice or crispy noodles, spring rolls and prawn crackers.
- Duck dishes, meat with visible fat, and poultry with skin on.
- Sticky spare ribs and sweet-and-sour dishes.

Healthier alternatives:

- Stir-fried vegetable dishes (with or without bean curd, chicken or prawns).
- Steamed dim sums.
- Grilled fish dishes.
- Boiled rice and boiled noodles.

Be Menu savvy

- Choose grilled, baked, poached or steamed chicken breast, fish and shellfish, as they will be lower in fat.
- Select tomato-based sauces, instead of high-fat cheese or cream sauces.
- Ask for dressings, gravy and sauces to be served separately – that way you can add as little as you want.
- Ask to have your vegetables served without butter or cream, and salads without dressing – you can save a lot of fat and calories that way.
- Choose a starter or a dessert that you can share. That way you can still have a treat, just a smaller portion of it.
- Choose rice or a jacket potato to have with your meal rather than chips.
- Choose a vitamin-packed fruit salad or a sorbet for a dessert – both are fat-free.
- Order a starter as your main course and ask for it to be served with a large salad or plain vegetables.
- Listen to your body and don't be afraid to leave food on your plate. Also ask for your plate to be removed as soon as you have finished so you are not tempted to continue to nibble.
- Try to avoid or limit alcohol – it can make you relax so much that you lose sight of your healthy eating habits.
- Don't be tempted by the savoury nibbles that may be offered while you are waiting for your meal to arrive.
- Don't assume that a vegetarian option will be lower in fat – always check. Many have creamy or cheesy sauces that are full of fat.
- Don't be tempted to order more food than you need. If you notice that portions being served to diners on other tables are larger than you would like, ask if you can have a smaller portion when you order. Likewise, if side salads appear small, ask for a larger one.
- Eat slowly – it'll give your stomach a chance to get the 'I'm full' message to your brain.
- Enjoy the conversation and experience.

Healthy eating quiz

If you were presented with this menu in a restaurant could you pick the healthiest starter, main course and dessert? Answers at the bottom of the page.

1 Starters

a Deep-fried garlic mushrooms
b Orange and grapefruit salad
c Pâté with toast and cranberry jelly
d Battered goujons of plaice

2 Main course

a Steak and stout pie with puff pastry crust
b Gammon steak with peach and pineapple
c Pan-fried chicken with chips, tomatoes and mushrooms
d Vegetable lasagne

3 Dessert

a Summer fruit pudding with raspberry coulis
b Sticky toffee pudding with vanilla custard
c Black Forest Gateau with cream
d Deep-filled apple and caramel pie

ITALIAN:

The 'baddies':

- Deep-pan and stuffed-crust pizzas.
- Toppings which include salami, pepperoni, other processed meats or extra cheese.
- Creamy pasta dishes like carbonara, lasagne and cannelloni.
- Garlic bread.

Healthier alternatives:

- Wholemeal pizza bases or dough.
- Toppings with mushrooms, peppers, onions, sweet corn, chicken, prawns, ham and tuna. Ask for less cheese.
- Pasta with tomato-based sauces.

FISH AND CHIPS:

The 'baddies':

- Fried fish (battered or breaded).
- Anything else that's battered or breaded.
- Fried chips.
- Pies, pasties, frankfurters or sausages.

Healthier alternatives:

- Only eat the fish – leave the batter.
- If you must have chips, try sweet potato chips or wedges as an alternative.

BURGER BARS:

The 'baddies':

- Burgers and buns.
- Fries.
- Mayonnaise.
- Creamy dressings.

Healthier alternatives:

- If you simply must have a burger, ask for it without the bun and sit it on a large salad with a low-fat sauce or a squeeze of lemon.

Many of the large burger chains are getting the nutritional message, and now produce nutritional information. But read it carefully – the salad may be fine, but the dressing could be packed with fat – ask if you could have it without.

CREATE THE TAKEAWAY TASTE

You can create a healthy takeaway night for family and friends in your own kitchen.

Burgers: Make your own burgers using lean beef, lamb or chicken, with onions and seasonings, and grill them slowly. Serve with a crunchy salad, low-fat mayonnaise and tasty relishes and salsa.

Fish and chips: Instead of battered fish, buy fillets of fish from your fishmonger or supermarket and make your own crispy crumb. Dip the fillets in lightly beaten egg white seasoned with mustard powder, garlic or freshly chopped herbs and then into grated wholemeal breadcrumbs or crushed cornflakes. Place on baking parchment, spray with a little oil, and bake in the oven until the fish is cooked and the coating crisp.

ANSWERS: Orange and grapefruit salad, gammon steak with peach and pineapple, summer fruit pudding with raspberry coulis

To make home-made chunky chips, peel some sweet potatoes, cut into fat chips and parboil for a minute or two. Drain and lightly spray with oil. Bake in the oven at medium heat (180°C/Gas 4) for half an hour until they are brown and crispy. Turn several times while they are cooking.

Serve your fish and chips with grilled tomatoes and peas or a colourful salad.

Pizza: Make or buy a wholemeal pizza base and construct your own topping. First make a thick tomato and basil sauce and then choose any topping you like. The secret of a healthy pizza is to go easy on the cheese. Try using ricotta, which is naturally low in fat – if you need extra taste, sprinkle a little strongly flavoured Parmesan on the pizza when it comes out of the oven. Serve with a lightly dressed green salad.

TRAVEL SNACKS

If you're going on a car journey, especially with children, leave the sweets, fizzy drinks, crisps and biscuits at home and stock up with healthy snacks instead. Try taking a selection from the following:

- A large plastic box filled with apple slices, orange segments, pear slices and grapes. Toss the apple and pear slices in a little lemon juice to prevent them discolouring.
- A large plastic box filled with plain popcorn.
- A bag of trail mix or mixed nuts and seeds.
- Bottled still water.
- Some small squares of home-made energy bar.

If you are going on a long journey, take along a picnic, rather than taking a break at a service station. If you choose a stopping place where there is a convenient play park, the children will be able to let off steam, and might even sleep for the next stage of the journey.

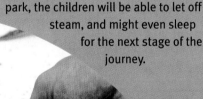

Home-made Energy bar

This nutty, fruity bar provides slow-release energy.

150g porridge oats
½ tsp cinnamon
75g low-fat spread
3tbsp set honey
2tbsp water
50g walnuts, roughly chopped
25g pumpkin seeds
25g sunflower seeds
25g desiccated coconut
75g raisins or sultanas
5 'ready to eat' dried apricots, roughly chopped
3 dates, roughly chopped
10g sesame seeds

1 Preheat the oven.

2 Melt the low-fat spread, honey and water in a large saucepan over a low heat. Cook for 3–4 minutes, stirring continuously, until it resembles a thick sauce.

3 Add all the remaining ingredients and stir to mix thoroughly.

4 Line a 30x19cm Swiss roll tin with nonstick baking parchment.

5 Spoon the mixture into the tin and flatten the surface.

6 Bake for 25–30 minutes until the mixture is firm to the touch and a light golden colour.

7 Remove from the oven, loosen the edges with a knife and leave to cool for 10 minutes.

8 Mark the bar into small squares and cut. Store in an airtight tin.

ACTION
IN THE SWIM

Swimming is a great all-round exercise, giving your heart and lungs a workout

Swimming is one of the best forms of exercise to improve general fitness. As an aerobic exercise, it helps to strengthen the lungs, heart and circulatory system. Swimming is often recommended by the medical profession to sportsmen and women, and others who are recovering from injuries or who suffer from pain, especially arthritic pain. It's also a good exercise during pregnancy (see also November's chapter, page 182).

Why not add a couple of trips to the pool to your weekly exercise plan? There are often special 'early bird' sessions you can attend before work or adults-only evening sessions. If you haven't been swimming for a long time start gradually and work up to twenty or thirty minutes a couple of times a week.

And if you can't swim, why not learn? It's never too late!

Most town leisure centres and pools run swimming classes for adults, or just for ladies, so it shouldn't be too difficult to find one. Learning to swim is very satisfying, and with practice it doesn't take long to become a confident swimmer. If your children can't swim, why not find a class for them too?

If you're not ready to learn to swim straight away, try aquarobics. Water is a thousand times denser than air and provides twelve times the resistance you get from doing the same exercises on land.

Raj Mann

Raj Mann was a 27-year-old market analyst who lived with his wife and young family in Warwick. At five foot eight, he weighed 22 stone.

Raj was the ultimate sneaky eater. Even though his wife, Dali, cooked fresh, healthy meals for the family every evening, Raj usually stopped off for a takeaway on his way home before dinner. That's after he had spent all day snacking on chocolate and drinking gallons of sugary tea at work, and he usually had a pub lunch.

And even that wasn't enough. Raj was such a snack-a-holic that he had his own freezer out in the garage where he hid all sorts of goodies such as chips and pizzas. At night, when the family were in bed, he would sit and munch in front of the TV.

Raj's family had no idea of the extent of his secret eating habits and Gillian McKeith was there to blow the whistle on this sneaky eater. When she raided the kitchen she was initially pleased to see the fridge full of the fresh and healthy food Dali used for the family meals, but that soon changed when Raj confessed and showed her the other freezer in the garage.

Gillian confronted Raj and Dali with all the food that Raj had eaten behind Dali's back. Gillian had strong words for Raj, telling him that he was insulting Dali by preferring to eat this to the beautiful meals she prepared. She illustrated the amount of fat Raj got through in a typical week – by showing him five kilos of animal fat.

Raj's blood test confirmed that his cholesterol level was 6.8 – a healthy level is 5 or below.

Gillian devised a new regime for Raj comprising three healthy main meals and healthy snacks with lots of juices. His new low-carb, high-protein diet was full of fish, grains, fruit and vegetables designed to curb his hunger and lower his cholesterol. Gillian also put the freezer in the garage under lock and key!

Initially Raj struggled with temptation from the takeaways on the way home. The miso soup that Gillian prescribed didn't go down well either, and he missed the food in the freezer. Gillian showed him alternative ways of introducing exciting flavours into foods by using lots of herbs and ingredients such as nori flakes. She also introduced him to gentle exercise to build up his fitness without straining his heart.

By week six, Raj was seeing results and finding the diet easier and easier. He even made Dali a healthy meal of chickpea burgers. He began going to the gym regularly and even started to play football again.

When Gillian returned at the end of the two months she was delighted to see the new Raj. He had lost three and a half stone and was bursting with energy and enthusiasm. As he said in a text he recently sent to Gillian, he now feels like a god and has the confidence and energy to do anything.

CASE STUDY

MENU PLANNER
AUGUST IDEAS

 **AUGUST BEST BUYS**

Make the most of:

Strawberries

Raspberries

Plums

Aubergines

Peppers

Courgettes

Sweet corn

Gooseberries

Peas

Figs

Lettuce

Salad onions

Menu 1

Breakfast   Tofu and vegetable pan-fry

Lunch   Asian chicken salad

Dinner   Chinese-style steamed fish

Mixed summer fruit fool

Menu 2

Breakfast   Fruity oat breakfast

Lunch   Smoked trout and horseradish pâté

Dinner   Mediterranean lamb and courgette kebabs

Tropical fruit dessert

Menu 1
☼ Tofu and vegetable pan-fry

1 Deseed and thinly slice the pepper. Wipe and slice the mushrooms. Cut the tomatoes into eight pieces and finely slice the onions.
2 Lightly oil a frying pan or wok. Stir-fry the vegetables for 3 minutes.
3 Add the turmeric, water, tomato purée and marinated tofu pieces. Cook the stir-fry for a further 3–4 minutes.
4 Transfer to heated plates and garnish with parsley.

Health fact: A breakfast containing protein helps keep your energy levels up throughout the morning – and tofu is an excellent low-fat vegetarian source of protein.

100g marinated tofu

1 red pepper, deseeded and sliced

100g mushrooms, sliced

½ a red onion sliced

Pinch of turmeric

2 tomatoes, cut into eight pieces

2tbsp water

1tbsp tomato purée

Ground black pepper

1tsp olive oil

4 sprigs parsley

Serves 4

☀ Asian chicken salad

1 medium carrot, peeled

½ a cucumber, halved lengthways

1 small red onion, peeled and halved

1 red pepper, quartered and deseeded

3 handfuls bean sprouts

Small handful fresh mint leaves (about 15g)

50g unsalted cashew nuts, roughly chopped

150g cooked, skinless chicken breast

For the dressing:

1tbsp sunflower or groundnut oil

1tsp tamari soy sauce

1tsp sesame oil

1tsp finely grated fresh root ginger

1 small garlic clove, peeled and crushed

Freshly squeezed juice of 1 lime

Serves 4

1 Grate the carrot, cucumber and onion. Slice the red pepper. Tip the vegetables into a bowl.

2 Wash and drain the bean sprouts and mint leaves, and add to the prepared vegetables. Toss in the chopped cashews.

3 Spoon the salad onto 4 plates.

4 Tear the chicken into shreds and place on top of the salads. Place the dressing ingredients in a small, screw-top jar. Fasten the lid and shake well. Pour a little of the dressing over each of the salads and serve.

> **Health fact:** As well as providing a wonderful, exotic taste, ginger contains aromatic substances which help prevent nausea – if you or your children suffer from travel sickness, try chewing a piece of crystallised ginger.

Grated fresh ginger also makes a soothing tea when you've got a cold – steep in hot water and add honey to taste.

Raspberries and strawberries are excellent sources of vitamin C and also contain a phytochemical called ellagic acid that is believed to help protect against cancer.

☽ Chinese-style steamed fish

1 Fill a steamer with cold water. Remove any tiny bones from the fish with tweezers, if necessary.
2 Place the fish fillets on a large piece of foil and lift the sides up all around it to make a shallow bowl to hold the marinade. Mix the soy sauce, ginger, garlic and spring onions in a small bowl. Pour over the fish and leave in a cool place for 10 minutes.
3 Turn the fish once or twice to coat in the marinade, leaving skin down. Fold the foil sides inwards and pinch together lightly to make a loose parcel. Place in the centre of the steamer basket, making sure that steam can rise through the steam vents around the parcel.
4 Spread the vegetables evenly around the fish and put the lid on top. Steam for about 15 minutes until the fish is cooked and the vegetables are tender. Divide the vegetables between 2 plates and carefully place the fish fillets on top. Peel off the skin and spoon the cooking juices over to serve.

> **Health fact:** Mackerel and trout are packed with essential omega-3 fatty acids. Most people don't eat enough omega-3s – try to include oily fish in your diet at least twice a week (but no more if you are pregnant).

2 fresh mackerel or trout fillets, each about 125g

300g bag vegetable and bean sprout stir-fry mix

For the marinade:

1tbsp organic tamari soy sauce

2.5cm piece fresh root ginger, peeled and cut into matchstick-sized pieces

1 garlic clove, peeled and thinly sliced

3 spring onions, trimmed and sliced

Serves 2

Mixed summer fruit fool

1 Wash and hull the strawberries, then cut in half. Wash the raspberries and drain well. Pat dry on kitchen paper.
2 Purée half of the strawberries and raspberries plus the banana in a bowl with a stick blender or in a liquidiser. Tip the yogurt into a bowl and gently stir in 3tbsp of the fruit sauce.
3 Spoon the reserved strawberries and raspberries, fruit sauce and the yogurt mixture alternately into pretty glasses or dessert dishes. Eat at once or chill for up to 3 hours before serving. Decorate with fresh mint leaves, if liked.

TIP
● You can use any soft summer berries for this quick dessert (even frozen berries work well if they are defrosted and thoroughly drained before use).
● If you can't find 0%-fat Greek yogurt, use plain fat-free bio-yogurt or virtually fat-free fromage frais instead.

250g fresh strawberries

150g fresh raspberries

1 large banana thickly sliced

1 pot (150g) 0%-fat Greek yogurt

Fresh mint leaves, to decorate

Serves 4

Menu 2
☀ Fruity oat breakfast

175g organic or jumbo porridge oats

75g sultanas

75g raisins

75g 'no soak' dried apricots, quartered

75g sunflower seeds

75g pumpkin seeds

75g flaked almonds

Skimmed milk, 0%-fat Greek yogurt or natural bio-yogurt and fresh berries, to serve

Makes 8 servings

1   Combine all the dry ingredients and spoon the required servings into bowls – around 3 heaped dessertspoons should be enough for each person.
2   Serve with skimmed milk or top with yogurt and fresh berries. Store any remaining oat mixture in a covered container in a cool, dark place for up to 2 weeks.

TIP
•   Add a ready-prepared combination of seeds and dried fruit to the oats if you prefer.

This breakfast provides good sources of magnesium, which helps to keep the heart healthy. It also contains zinc, which is important for a healthy immune system, and iron, needed for healthy red blood cells.

☼ Smoked trout and horseradish pâté

2x125g pack skinless hot-smoked trout

6tbsp 0%-fat Greek yogurt or fat-free bio-yogurt

Finely grated zest of a lemon

2–3tsp hot horseradish sauce, preferably organic

Freshly ground black pepper

Serves 4

1 Place the trout, yogurt, lemon zest and horseradish sauce in a food processor. Season with a little ground black pepper.

2 Blend for 10 seconds, then remove the lid and push the mixture down with a spatula. Replace the lid and blend until the mixture forms a smooth, thick paste.

3 Remove the blade and spoon the pâté into a small dish. Eat at once, or cover and chill for up to 24 hours before serving.

4 Serve with hot wholegrain toast or rye crackers, lemon wedges for squeezing and a salad garnish.

Health fact: Adding horseradish gives the pâté a kick and cuts down on the need to add salt – adults should eat a maximum 6g of salt (2.4g sodium) per day.

TIP

- You can use any hot-smoked fish you like for this recipe – mackerel and salmon are good alternatives. Just keep the basic quantities the same. This recipe can also easily be doubled or trebled, and makes a delicious, healthy starter when entertaining.

☾ Mediterranean lamb and courgette kebabs

1 Ideally at least 4 hours before cooking (and up to 24 hours), put the olive oil, lemon juice, garlic, cumin, mint or oregano, and pepper to taste in a bowl large enough to hold the lamb pieces and stir together. Add the lamb pieces and stir around. Cover and chill until 20 minutes before cooking, stirring occasionally to coat the lamb.

2 Meanwhile, bring a small pan of water to the boil. Add the pepper chunks and blanch for 1 minute. Drain and rinse in cold water to stop the cooking, then pat dry and set aside.

3 Light the barbecue coals and leave them to become glowing. Position the rack about 10cm above the coals and lightly grease with olive oil. (Alternatively, preheat the grill to high, lightly grease the grill rack with olive oil and position it 10cm below the heat.) Lightly grease 4 long (or 8 short) flat metal kebab skewers with olive oil.

4 Thread the lamb, peppers, courgettes and spring onions onto the skewers, dividing the ingredients as evenly as possible.

5 Place the skewers on the rack and barbecue for 10–15 minutes, turning them frequently and basting with the remaining marinade, until lightly charred but leaving the meat still pink inside. Serve hot with lemon wedges for squeezing over.

½ tbsp fruity olive oil, plus extra for greasing the spears and rack

Juice of 2 lemons

2 large garlic cloves, crushed

½ tsp ground cumin

1 tbsp chopped fresh mint or oregano

Freshly ground black pepper

500g boneless lamb fillet or leg, well trimmed and cut into 2.5cm slices

2 green or red peppers, deseeded and cut into 4cm chunks

2 medium courgettes, trimmed and cut into 1cm slices

4 thick spring onions, each cut into 6 pieces

Lemon wedges, to garnish

Serves 4

Tropical fruit dessert

1 Top and tail the pineapple and carefully remove all the skin with a sharp knife. Cut into quarters lengthways and remove the tough central core. Cut the pineapple flesh into chunky pieces and place in a blender.

2 Stand the mango on a chopping board and carefully cut either side of the large, flat stone using a sharp knife. Scoop out the flesh, away from the flesh and stone, with a dessertspoon and place in the blender.

3 Add the bananas and water. Blend on low for a few seconds, then switch to high and blend until smooth.

4 Peel the papaya then cut in half and discard the seeds. Cut the flesh into small pieces. Divide the papaya between 4 plates. Pour over the mango and pineapple sauce. Finish with spoonfuls of bio-yogurt and a little shredded coconut, if liked.

1 small pineapple

1 ripe mango

2 bananas, peeled and thickly sliced

125ml cold water

1 ripe papaya

Fat-free bio-yogurt and shredded coconut, to serve (optional)

Serves 4

september

HEALTHY PACKED LUNCHES FOR KIDS AND GROWN-UPS

There's no need for a packed lunch to be a boring and predictable affair – with a little planning, you can have a healthy feast.

The healthy lunchbox

Lunch should provide both adults and children with approximately one third of their daily energy requirements as well as a third of their protein, carbohydrate, fibre, vitamin and mineral needs.

Try to include:

- At least one portion of fruit (preferably fresh, or alternatively a small quantity of dried fruit)
- At least one portion of salad or vegetables
- One protein food (meat, chicken, fish, eggs, or a vegetarian alternative)
- One dairy or calcium-rich food (yogurt, milk, low-fat cheese)
- One carbohydrate food (wholemeal bread, wholemeal pasta, rice, wholewheat noodles)
- Water or pure fruit juice (diluted for children)

✔ THIS MONTH, MAKE SURE YOU:

- Make it yourself – don't rely on processed foods
- Get your finger on the pulse – increase the amount of beans, lentils and wholegrain foods in your diet

If you're aiming for a healthy lifestyle, working through lunch is one bad habit you need to try to break. Not only does a nutritious lunch provide you with the energy to get through the afternoon, but you are also less likely to reach for a packet of crisps or a chocolate bar to keep you going.

When you're at work it's a good idea to try to get away from your desk and relax while you eat your lunch. Perhaps combine lunch with a walk in the park or some window-shopping. If you have a workplace canteen check out the healthy options – if there aren't any, raise it with the management.

Most people who work away from home take a packed lunch or slip out for a bite to eat. If you buy a sandwich or salad at lunchtime look for the healthy options, steer clear of the high-fat mayo and check any other dressings, not only for the fat content but also the salt. You may be lucky enough to find a sandwich bar where sandwiches are made to order, so you can pick your filling from the wide array of protein foods and salad vegetables on offer. You will be able to ask what is in their dressings and forgo those high in fat. You could also ask them to go easy on the spread, or leave it out if you're choosing a moist filling. If you buy a pasta or rice salad, always read the label carefully, as some are very high in fat or salt.

It's often cheaper – and healthier – to pack your own lunchbox. But don't get into a rut and resort to bringing the same boring items day after day, or you could be tempted to reach for the biscuits. This is one meal where you really can be adventurous without having to take the tastes of other members of the family into account. So give your culinary know-how free rein and tantalise your taste buds.

As well as tucking into the healthy lunchboxes we're going to be suggesting for the younger members of the family, why not dream up your own lunch ideas?

The variety of sandwiches, wraps and meal salads you can make are almost endless, and you can always make use of leftovers from last night's dinner – or cook a little extra.

- Cold home-made chicken curry and rice on a bed of salad vegetables is delicious.
- A little cold chicken or vegetable curry mixed with a tablespoon of low-fat yogurt makes a quick filling for a fajita wrap, roll or sandwich.
- Or how about a little leftover Bolognese sauce mixed into couscous?

CHILDREN'S LUNCHBOXES

Surveys of children's packed lunches have found many children bringing to school lunchboxes full of chocolate bars, white-bread sandwiches, high-fat and high-salt processed snacks, and fizzy drinks. A recent survey by the Food Standards Agency found that nine out of ten children's lunches contained too many fatty and sugary foods, and many are high in salt too.

But providing a healthy lunchbox for your children is simple. It doesn't need to be time-consuming or break the bank.

It *is* possible to avoid processed and ready-made options, and by packing your own lunchbox instead of resorting to shop-bought products, you can save money, and have peace of mind.

The most important things to remember when packing a child's lunchbox are that it needs to be nourishing and enjoyable and, in their eyes, 'cool'.

Try to keep them interested in lunch by ringing the changes. Make treats, like crisps and cakes, very occasional, and when you do use them, select the healthier products.

Let the children have some say in what goes into their lunchboxes – within your guidelines. Tell them what is available, and encourage them to get involved in the preparation. Persuade them to invent their own fillings for sandwiches and wraps – it gives them a sense of responsibility and encourages them to make healthy decisions for themselves. But be ready to offer guidance if suggested combinations are too 'way out'. Salmon and strawberry jam, anyone?

The next time you're in the supermarket, take a careful look at the pre-packaged lunchbox foods aimed at children. Sadly, some of them are high in fat, sugar or salt. There is no doubt that their packaging and presentation do appeal to children, but luckily it's easy to pack the same type of snack food, but using healthier choices. Remember, if you do buy cooked meats, avoid the highly processed meats in favour of the simple 'baked' or 'roasted' joints.

Don't worry if your child wants to eat the same filling in their sandwiches every day. It is more important that they *do* eat them. If their choice is for a filling which doesn't contain protein – such as jam or honey – it's simple to provide some protein separately, such as stir-fried chicken strips, a couple of sticks of cheese, or some cottage cheese and pineapple in a small pot.

Keep lunchbox food simple to eat with fingers or a spoon. Don't be too adventurous – this isn't the time to introduce unfamiliar items. They are more likely to eat their lunch if it resembles the food their friends are eating, albeit a healthy version. The risk of teasing because they've got 'weird food' is a sure-fire way to discourage them from wanting to open their lunchbox in front of other children.

Fortunately the widespread popularity of such items as pitta breads, baguettes and wraps, means that you're no longer limited to the old lunchbox faithful, the sandwich.

LUNCHBOX WINNERS

Here are just a few ways to add variety to a child's lunchbox (and to your own):

Bread: Use wholemeal or granary bread if possible, but if children say they don't like it, use one of the new high-fibre 'white' loaves. You could also use one slice of white bread and one slice of brown as a compromise.

Vary the type of bread you use and try wraps, pittas, mini-pittas, bagels, rolls or English muffins. Experiment with some of the more exciting breads such as granary, walnut, sun-dried tomato, raisin or wholemeal cheese bread – but give these a trial run at the weekend before adding them to the lunchbox, in case the child doesn't want to eat it.

Avoid the morning rush by preparing lunchboxes the night before – then everyone can help. You can keep the lunches in the fridge until the morning.

Nut allergies

If your child suffers from a nut allergy, you'll obviously know not to give him or her sandwiches containing peanut butter, or other nut butters. But make sure to warn your child not to swap sandwiches or other foods with friends who might have lunches containing nuts.

Simple soup

To make four portions of soup you need:

1 carrot, finely diced
1 medium potato, peeled and diced
1 small leek, washed and finely sliced
A couple of broccoli florets or cauliflower florets
1 vegetable low-salt stock cube, or vegetable bouillon powder
900 ml water
50g red lentils
Freshly ground black pepper.

1. Place all of the prepared vegetables in a large saucepan and bring to the boil. Skim off any foam and reduce heat. Simmer the soup for 20 minutes until the vegetables are tender.

2. Remove some of the cooked vegetables (about 2 heaped slotted spoonfuls) to a bowl. Pour the remainder of the soup into a blender and blend until almost smooth. Pour the blended soup, and the reserved vegetables back into the saucepan. Reheat the soup and serve or put into a warmed vacuum flask.

Fillings: Include a protein-rich food in the fillings, such as fish, chicken, lean meat, cheese or peanut butter, and some salad (lettuce, cucumber or tomato).

Here are a few fillings you might like to try:
Low-fat soft cheese with finely sliced dried apricot or grated carrot
Low-fat soft cheese, sliced banana and a drizzle of runny honey
Spicy stir-fried chicken and crispy lettuce and pepper strips
Roasted Mediterranean vegetables and salad leaves
Sliced poached chicken breast, low-fat yogurt and finely chopped salad vegetables
Tomato, lettuce and mozzarella cheese
Salmon, chopped cucumber and low-fat mayonnaise
Chopped hard-boiled egg, cress and low-fat mayonnaise
Peanut butter and banana
Chopped chicken, tossed in a little fromage frais, with salad
Turkey and low-fat coleslaw
Grated cheese with apple slices
Drained cottage cheese, grated carrot and grated apple
Tuna, sweet corn and pepper

To avoid soggy sandwiches, dry any salad vegetables well after washing them. Go easy on the spread, or use low-fat yogurt, or a scraping of finely chopped pickle or chutney.

Or try a wholemeal roll and a chicken drumstick separately, or some rolled slices of lean ham, and cherry tomatoes.

NON-SANDWICH ALTERNATIVES

Some children, particularly older ones, are more willing to consider alternatives to sandwiches in their lunchboxes.

On cold days they might welcome some home-made soup in a flask, plus a crusty bread roll. Vegetable and lentil soup is quick, easy to make, and filling. You can vary the vegetables you use to make the soup depending on what you have available.

Lunchbox salads

Especially during the summer, salads are light and refreshing and also full of essential vitamins or minerals.

Here are five protein-rich summer salad ideas for a lunchbox:
- Lettuce, sliced tomato, cucumber and spring onion, topped with cottage cheese and two or three peach slices
- Bean sprouts, shredded carrot, cucumber strips and shredded lettuce topped with stir-fried chicken strips (seasoned during cooking with a little Chinese spice powder) or marinated tofu
- Lettuce, beetroot, tomato and orange segments topped with crumbled cheese

- Lettuce, tomato, low-fat or home-made coleslaw, topped with two small slices of lean ham
- Lettuce, halved cherry tomatoes, grated carrot, thinly sliced radishes, topped with drained flaked tuna in water or brine

All of the salads can be lightly dressed with a drizzle of fat-free salad dressing or a teaspoon of low-fat mayonnaise or salad cream.

Add a tablespoon of nuts and seeds for extra crunch and protein. Cold sliced new potatoes (cooked with their skins on to retain nutrients) make a tasty addition to a meal salad.

Rice or lentil salads are also simple to prepare and nutritious – they're high in fibre, low-GI complex carbohydrates, and vitamins, especially folate and other B-vitamins. Cook some brown rice or lentils, add some diced salad vegetables, and a little cooked turkey or chicken, then toss in a light dressing.

Pasta salads are another good lunchbox option. Try pasta with tuna, pepper and sweet corn, or cooked chicken, sweet tomato, cherry tomato and torn baby spinach leaves. If you're having a pasta meal in the evening, cook a couple of extra portions to chill and make into pasta salads.

A slice of home-made vegetable quiche – if you buy a quiche look for the healthy option that's lower in salt and fat – or a slice of Spanish omelette (sometimes called a tortilla) is also popular. Both of these could be prepared for the evening meal and slices saved for the next day's lunchboxes.

Home-made pizza is another favourite with children. Prepare a large one together for the evening meal, letting the children choose some of the toppings, and save slices for their lunchboxes. Make a thick tomato and vegetable sauce to spread over the base then top with a selection of thinly chopped or sliced vegetables – peppers, tomato, mushrooms, courgettes, onion – some small pieces of chicken, ham or tuna, and a little crumbled mozzarella or grated half-fat cheese.

As an alternative to the ubiquitous sandwich, try wraps, bagels, salads or soup in a flask.

Bagel chips

Simply slice bagels – wholemeal if available – horizontally into thin rounds. Lightly brush the surfaces with olive oil (you can flavour it with a little garlic or chilli paste) and then bake in a slow oven (150°C/Gas 2) until they are lightly toasted and crisp. Keep an eye on them so they don't burn. They'll keep in an airtight tin for two or three days without losing their crispness.

Fruit and vegetables

Children are more likely to eat fruit and vegetables in their lunchboxes if they are small and easy to eat.

Try including one of these:
A small apple
An easy-peel clementine or satsuma
Low-fat dip and some vegetable sticks
Small packs of dried fruit
A handful of sugar snap peas
A small fruit smoothie
Cherry tomatoes
A small pot of fruit in juice
A pot of fresh fruit slices
A handful of grapes
2 fresh apricots
A halved kiwi fruit (don't forget to put a spoon in the lunchbox so they can eat it like a boiled egg)

Dairy and calcium-rich foods

Include a dairy food, such as cheese, yogurt, fromage frais or a calcium-enriched soya alternative, to provide the calcium need to build healthy bones. Nuts (especially almonds) and tinned sardines and salmon, are also sources of calcium.

Treats

Everyone likes a treat now and again so there's no need to ban them from the lunchbox. Just limit them and replace the chocolate bars and cakes with:
- Scones, currant buns or fruit bread
- Malt loaf, oatcakes, home-made flapjack
- A piece of healthy recipe fruit cake

If you bake at home for lunchboxes, look for recipes that are lower in fat and add a little less sugar. You can often cut down on the sugar in a recipe if it includes fruit, or by adding a little banana, apple or apricot purée to increase the sweet taste. Make your own low-fat and low-sugar muffins – you can reduce the sugar and use mashed banana to sweeten them. And if your children love all things chocolate, flavour your baking with cocoa or 70%-cocoa drinking chocolate, to give the desired effect.

If you want to use jam in sandwiches or in cakes, choose one with reduced sugar.

When you buy crisps select the low-fat and low-salt versions and keep them as very occasional treats. Also look for alternatives like plain popcorn or pretzels. Another idea is to make your own bagel chips – they're low-fat and delicious.

Drinks

Avoid fizzy drinks and include water, diluted fruit juice or milk in the lunchbox.

Add an ice pack to the lunch box, or freeze the drink, to keep the food cool. If you choose sandwich fillings that can be frozen, you can take the sandwiches out of the freezer at breakfast time and they will gradually defrost during the morning.

CHECK OUT SCHOOL DINNERS

If your children have school dinners, ask them what they are eating. It's important that you know. If they choose their own school lunches discuss the benefits of selecting healthy options.

There have been some important changes to school meals regulations recently and schools are being required to provide more healthy options. But the problem is that in many cases some of the less healthy are still available alongside the healthy choices. Where a cafeteria system is in operation, this means that children may still able to choose the chips and burgers more often than you would like.

If you're happy with the meals being served at your child's school, persuade them to give school dinners a try, even if it's not every day. Children are more likely to try unfamiliar foods if their friends are eating them.

If you're not happy with the meals being offered at lunchtime, speak to a school governor or the head teacher and get together with other parents to press for improvements to be made.

SUPER SPROUTED SEEDS

Just think about it – a sprout contains all the energy and nutrients needed to transform a small seed into a healthy plant. So is it really a wonder that sprouted seeds are so good for us?

Sprouts do not contain any additives and they're so quick and simple to grow at home. All the seeds need to sprout is water and air and within days you'll have a delicious, highly nutritious crop. To get sprouting all you'll need is a jam jar, a piece of muslin and an elastic band. How's that for easy gardening?

There is a sprout variety to suit every taste, from mild to hot, nutty to spicy and a wide range of ways to use them. Mung beans (Chinese bean sprouts), alfalfa, lentils and chickpeas are just a few that you might like to try. Add them to salads, stir-fries, soups, dips, casseroles and stews, or just nibble them on their own.

You'll find packets of seeds for sprouting at garden centres and health food shops. They all come with their own instructions.

ACTION
TOP OF THE CLASS

Have you ever wanted to know what's going on under the bonnet of the car? Have you ever dreamed of sitting by a river and creating a watercolour masterpiece? Or dancing a sassy salsa? Or brushing up on your French conversation?

With the new school year beginning, why not find time to get back into the classroom to learn something new? It's challenging, fun, and you're sure to make some new friends. It will also give you a couple of hours a week away from your home or work responsibilities.

The range of classes available is constantly growing so you're sure to find something to interest you. As well as evening classes there are also a wide range of daytime and one-day Saturday classes. Many of the establishments who organise daytime classes also have crèches.

Career minded

Why not take a course that could improve your career prospects? Or perhaps you've taken a career break, and want to get back into work.

There are a variety of courses available, from technical colleges, schools and universities, whether you want to start from the basics or simply improve your skills. The largest variety of courses is probably in Information Technology subjects, but if computers aren't your thing, you could try a vocational subject, such as hairdressing, jewellery making or plumbing. You may also be able to get a grant to help pay for your fees.

Down to business

A course could be just the impetus you need to set you on the road to starting your own business. Although it's an undeniably tough world out there, there's a lot of help and advice available for new business start-ups – your library is a good first port of call to find some useful contacts.

Helping hands

A good cause you support might need collectors, or you could ask your local charity shops whether they need anyone to serve customers or sort goods.

Look out for events and appeals in the local press, and ask if they need any helpers. Volunteering is a great way to make friends!

Hobbies and clubs

Look in your library or local newspaper for hobby clubs. Whether you're interested in investing on the stock market, keeping bees, amateur dramatics or photography, you'll probably find like-minded people living nearby.

If there isn't a club in the area for the subject that interests you, try starting your own! How about a reading circle, a music appreciation or knitting group?

MENU PLANNER
SEPTEMBER IDEAS

 **SEPTEMBER BEST BUYS**

Make the most of:

Apples

Plums

Damsons

Blackberries

Sweet corn

Spinach

Onions

Menu 1

Breakfast — Melon basket with grapes and yogurt

Lunch — Carrot, courgette and bean salad

Dinner — Mediterranean-style chicken breasts

Zesty apple and plum crunch

Menu 2

Breakfast — Sardines and tomatoes on a wholemeal muffin

Lunch — Tuna and mixed bean salad with pitta bread

Dinner — Turkey and leek burgers with tomato and avocado salsa

Apples and pears in spiced red wine

Menu 1
☀ Melon basket with grapes and yogurt

2 small ripe melons

175g red seedless grapes, washed

Juice of 1 lime

2x150ml low-fat natural yogurt

2tbsp toasted sunflower and pumpkin seeds

Serves 4

1 Cut the melons in half, remove the seeds and discard. Chop the flesh into bite-sized pieces.
2 Combine the melon flesh, the grapes and the lime juice in a bowl. Spoon into the 4 empty melon skins.
3 Top with natural yogurt and seeds and serve.

Health fact: Sunflower and pumpkin seeds are a great source of the mineral zinc, essential for a strong immune system.

☼ Carrot, courgette and bean salad

100g green beans, trimmed and halved

1 round or small iceberg lettuce

2 medium carrots, peeled

1 medium courgette, trimmed

1 can (400g) 'no-salt' red kidney beans, drained and rinsed

4 spring onions, trimmed and sliced

For the dressing:

3tbsp virgin olive oil

1tbsp cider vinegar or white wine vinegar

1tbsp finely chopped fresh parsley

1 garlic clove, peeled and crushed

½ tsp Dijon mustard

Freshly ground black pepper

Serves 4

1 Bring a small pan of water to the boil. Add the green beans and return to the boil. Cook for 2 minutes then drain in a colander under cold running water; set aside.
2 Wash and dry the lettuce and arrange on a large plate. Grate the carrots and courgette into the bowl. Add the green beans, kidney beans and spring onions.
3 Place the dressing ingredients in a small screw-top jar and season with a little ground black pepper. Fasten the lid and shake well. Pour over the bean salad and toss well together. Spoon the bean salad over the lettuce leaves and serve.

Health fact: Courgettes are a good source of the antioxidant vitamin C and provide useful amounts of B1, B6 and folate.

TIP
Serve this recipe just as it is, or add some lean cooked chicken or fish. Soft goats' cheese or feta also tastes great crumbled over the salad.

☽ Mediterranean-style chicken

1 Fill a steamer with cold water. Place the pine nuts in a small pan and cook over a medium heat for 2–3 minutes until lightly toasted, stirring regularly. Set aside. Cut roughly a quarter of each pepper into thin slices and cut the remainder into 2.5cm pieces; set aside.
2 Carefully cut each chicken breast horizontally three quarters of the way through the middle with a sharp knife to make a large pocket. Open out and fill the pockets with the sliced peppers, goats' cheese and pine nuts.
3 Close the pockets and brush the chicken with the pesto sauce. Place in a steamer basket. Put the lid on top and steam for about 20 minutes until the chicken is completely cooked and no pinkness remains.
4 Toss the salad leaves with the tomatoes and reserved peppers. Drizzle with a little balsamic vinegar and olive oil. Serve with the chicken.

> **Health fact:** Chicken meat is rich in protein, essential for growth and cell repair, and low in fat. It also provides important B-vitamins. The goats' cheese contains calcium which helps build healthy bones.

15g pine nuts

4 boneless chicken breasts (preferably free range or organic), each about 175g skinned

1 small red pepper, deseeded

1 small yellow pepper, deseeded

50g soft goats' cheese, cut into rough 1cm pieces

1tbsp red pesto sauce

1 bag mixed baby leaf salad

4 tomatoes, quartered

Balsamic vinegar and extra virgin olive oil, to serve

Serves 4

Zesty apple and plum crunch

1 Preheat the oven to 190°C/Gas 5. Peel the apples, cut into quarters and remove the core. Slice all of the apples.
2 Place the apple slices in a bowl and add the plums, orange juice, lemon zest and juice, sultanas and mixed spice. Toss well together then tip into a 1.4-litre pie dish.
3 Roughly chop the nuts and sprinkle over the top. Bake for 30–35 minutes until the apples are tender and the topping is pale golden brown. Serve warm or cold with 0%-fat Greek yogurt or fromage frais.

> **Health fact:** Apples are a good source of pectin – a type of soluble fibre that can help reduce high blood-cholesterol levels. They also contain potassium and the flavanoid quercetin, which has anti-cancer and anti-inflammatory actions.

4 apples

4 plums, stoned and quartered

Freshly squeezed juice of 1 orange

Finely grated zest and juice of 1 lemon

75g sultanas

½ tsp ground mixed spice

50g shelled mixed nuts

Serves 4

Beans have a low GI rating and are an excellent source of soluble fibre, as well as providing B-vitamins and protein. They are also a useful source of iron. The vitamin C from the tomatoes and lemon juice makes it easier for the body to absorb the iron from the beans.

Menu 2
☼ Sardines and tomatoes on a wholemeal muffin

1 Preheat the grill. Place the sardines on a plate. Mash them and add the Worcestershire sauce.
2 Grill the tomatoes and keep warm.
3 Split and toast the muffins. Divide the sardine topping between the 8 pieces of muffin and spread. Place under the grill until the topping is hot. Serve with the tomatoes.

2 tins (2 x 125g) sardines in tomato sauce

2 tsp Worcestershire sauce

4 wholemeal muffins

4 tomatoes, cut into slices or wedges

Serves 4

☀ Tuna and mixed bean salad with pitta bread

1 Empty the beans into a sieve and rinse under cold running water. Tip into a large serving bowl and add the tuna, tomatoes, chicory or little gem, red onion, garlic, oil, parsley and lemon juice and zest.
2 Toss together lightly and season to taste with ground black pepper. Split the pitta breads and fill with the tuna mixture or serve alongside the tuna and bean salad with a few fresh, green leaves.

TIPS
- This salad also tastes great when mixed with cooked chopped chicken instead of the tuna. Alternatively, for a highly nutritious vegetarian dish, leave the tuna out, and just add some coarsely grated carrot and courgette with a sprinkling of sesame seeds.
- Like the previous lunch salad, this recipe is also perfect as a packed lunch to take to work or school, and is brilliant for picnics too.

1 can (410g) 'no-salt' mixed canned beans

1 can (200g) tuna steak in spring water, drained

2 tomatoes, roughly chopped

2 chicory or 2 little gem lettuces, trimmed and sliced

1 small red onion, peeled and finely sliced

1 garlic clove, peeled and crushed

1tbsp extra virgin olive oil

3tbsp chopped fresh parsley

Freshly squeezed juice and finely grated or pared zest of 1 lemon

4 wholemeal pitta bread, warmed

Freshly ground black pepper

Serves 4

☽ Turkey and leek burgers with tomato and avocado salsa

1 small leek, trimmed and finely chopped (around 100g prepared weight)

1 small carrot, peeled and finely grated (around 100g prepared weight)

1 small onion, peeled and finely chopped (around 100g prepared weight)

1 garlic clove, peeled and crushed

500g minced turkey, preferably free-range or organic

2tsp organic vegetable bouillon (stock) powder

Freshly ground black pepper

¼ tsp sunflower oil, for greasing

Large mixed salad, to serve

For the salsa:

3 ripe tomatoes, chopped

2 spring onions, trimmed and finely sliced

½ a ripe avocado, stoned, peeled and chopped

Freshly squeezed juice of 1 lime or ½ a small lemon

2tbsp chopped fresh coriander or flat-leaf parsley

Serves 4

1 Place the leek, carrot, onion, garlic, turkey and bouillon powder in a bowl. Add a little ground black pepper and mix well. Lightly oil an electric health grill or ridged griddle pan and preheat.

2 Form the turkey mixture firmly into four balls with clean hands, then flatten into burger shapes and place on the grill or griddle. Grill for 4–5 minutes (if using an electric health grill, close the lid) until thoroughly cooked and no pinkness remains.

3 Toss the salsa ingredients together in a small bowl and season to taste with ground black pepper. Serve the burgers with the tomato and avocado salsa and a large salad.

Turkey meat is rich in protein – essential for growth and cell repair – and low in fat. It also provides important B-vitamins and tryptophan – an amino acid that could help keep your mood calm and balanced.

Apples and pears in spiced red wine

1. Put the wine, orange juice, sugar, cinnamon, allspice, ginger, cloves, star anise and juniper berries if liked in a saucepan over a high heat and bring to a boil. Continue boiling until the liquid is reduced to about 250ml.
2. Meanwhile, peel, halve, core and slice the pears. Peel, quarter, core and slice the apples and add them to the pear slices.
3. Reduce the heat under the wine to low, add the pear and apple pieces and poach for 3–5 minutes until they just start to feel tender when pierced with the tip of a knife. (They will continue to soften in the hot liquid.)
4. Transfer the fruit and syrup to a heatproof serving bowl. You can either serve warm or leave the fruit and syrup to cool, then cover and chill for up to a day. Use a spoon to remove the spices before serving. Serve sprinkled with the orange rind and a dollop of fromage frais or bio-yogurt, if liked.

Health fact: Apples provide the antioxidant quercetin and vitamin C, plus soluble fibre which can help lower cholesterol levels. Pears contain useful amounts of vitamin C, potassium and soluble fibre.

450ml red wine, such as Pinot Noir

Finely grated rind and juice of 1 large orange

1½ tbsp light brown muscovado sugar

¼ tsp ground allspice

1cm piece fresh root ginger, peeled and coarsely chopped

1 cinnamon stick, 7.5cm long, broken in half

4 cloves

2 star anise

4 juniper berries, lightly crushed (optional)

4 large ripe dessert pears

2 large apples

Virtually fat-free fromage frais or fat-free bio-yogurt, to serve (optional)

Serves 4

october

FEEDING CHILDREN – GROWING UP HEALTHILY

Childhood nutrition is a hot topic – and with good reason. Not only does healthy eating – or not – affect a child's wellbeing right now, it also impacts on his or her health in the future.

Childhood obesity is increasing, and conditions such as high blood pressure and type-2 diabetes, which were once only associated with adults, are being seen in younger and younger children.

But the story isn't all doom and gloom. By feeding our children nutritious meals, encouraging them to exercise, and showing them how to make healthy food choices, we can make a huge investment in their future good health and happiness.

YOUNG CHILDREN

The information in this chapter is only intended for children aged five and over, as younger children have more specialised nutritional needs. For nutritional advice for children aged four and under, contact your doctor or health visitor.

✔ **THIS MONTH, MAKE SURE YOU:**
- Banish the frying pan – and cut down the amount of saturated and trans fats in your family's diet
- Cut down on sugar and salt – reducing the amount of processed food you buy will really make a difference

TEN TIPS TO HELP CHILDREN TO EAT HEALTHILY

1 **Set a good example.** If you skip breakfast, eat lunch on the run and tuck into takeaways in front of the television, don't be surprised if your children want to do the same. They're more likely to make healthy choices if you do.

2 **Get the day off to a good start.** Always make time for breakfast, even if it means getting up fifteen minutes earlier and setting the table the night before. A healthy, sustaining breakfast not only improves concentration, but it also makes children less likely to want to snack on unhealthy foods during the morning. Beat boredom by ringing the changes at breakfast time:
- Add a portion of fresh fruit, and some seeds and nuts to a low-sugar cereal
- Top warmed Scotch pancakes with a tablespoon of set low-fat yogurt or fromage frais and some fresh or drained tinned fruit in juice
- Toast a bagel or wholemeal muffin and spread with low-fat soft cheese or yeast extract
- Make a high-energy fruit smoothie and a batch of healthy muffins
- Top wholemeal toast or rice cakes with cottage cheese and a sliced banana

3 **Don't hurry.** Give meals a high priority and set aside time so that they are not rushed affairs. Sitting down for a meal together gives you an opportunity to introduce 'new' foods in a non-confrontational way. Instead of adding them to a child's plate, when they are just as likely to say, 'What's this? I don't like it!' before a morsel has touched their lips, put a dish of the new food on the table – it could be mashed sweet potato, or some slices of plum, perhaps. Say that you spotted them when you were shopping and thought you'd all give them a try.

4 **Try, try and try again.** Don't be surprised if a child turns up his or her nose the first time a new food is offered; wait a while and try it again. It's been scientifically proven that in most cases if we try a food several times we do eventually develop a taste for it. But accept that children are no different from adults in that there will be some foods that they just do not like – ever. But with perseverance over the years, hopefully there will not be many.

5 **Think fruit and veg.** As fruits and vegetables come into season, try to introduce them into your children's diets. Show them new fruit and vegetables when you are in the supermarket and explain why it is important to eat them, as well as how yummy they are. Introduce them into meals, but if you find the children won't eat them cooked, offer them raw in salads or as crudités with a low-fat dip – many children prefer their veggies raw or lightly cooked and still crunchy.

If getting children to eat fruit and vegetables is a real issue in your household, you may have to resort to cunning, as a last resort, and sneak them into your children's meals. Although you're aiming to help them develop a taste for healthy foods, you still want to get these nutritious foods inside them somehow!

Add cooked, puréed carrots and other vegetables to pasta sauces, soups and stews, or add a banana to a smoothie or to a batch of healthy muffins. But don't give even the slightest hint to young children that they're on the five-a-day challenge or they'll quickly dig in their little heels and give you five reasons why they won't eat fruit and vegetables!

6 **Get label smart.** Read the labels on any tinned, processed and packaged food you buy for your children. Keep an eye open for 'hidden' salt, sugar and fat and bear in mind that a 'low fat' product may be packed with sugar. And try to avoid foods with ingredient lists as long as your arm – this generally means they're full of additives! As soon as children are old enough, get them interested in reading the labels and explain what they mean. It could even make shopping fun!

7 **Little chefs.** Encourage children to help in the kitchen. Let them choose a recipe, shop for the ingredients with you, and help you cook the dish. Start with quick and simple dishes like pasta with a sauce, tasty stir-fries, or low-sugar muffins for lunchboxes. Letting children help create dishes gives them a sense of achievement, encourages them to try new foods, shows them cooking is fun and sparks an interest in healthy eating

8 **Have a box of delights.** Limit the number of sweets and biscuits in the house and have a healthy treat box for children . . . and the adults. Fill it with healthy snacks such as unsalted nuts, dried fruit, plain popcorn, 'fruit leather', and mini rice cakes – and just the occasional chocolate bar or packet of sweets if you really must. Keep a stock of apples, oranges and bananas in the fruit bowl and a bowl of carrot, cucumber and pepper sticks in the fridge. Don't ban sweets, biscuits and cakes altogether. They then become 'forbidden fruit' and even more desirable. We all deserve a treat every now and again.

9 **Family mealtimes.** Make mealtimes relaxed and try to eat meals together at the table and not on trays in front of the television. Not only is it better for their digestion, it gives you all an opportunity to talk together.

10 **Don't panic.** Keep things in perspective. It's not a disaster that Callum won't eat his broccoli or Melanie thinks prunes are 'Yuk'. There are plenty of other healthy foods they can eat. Just do the best you can by providing them with a healthy balanced diet.

No one has yet found the secret of persuading children to eat everything put in front of them ... and they're not going to. So try to stay relaxed so that you all enjoy mealtimes.

WHAT CHILDREN NEED

By the time they start school, children need high-energy, nutritious diets because of their rapid growth spurts and all that running around. In fact they need a lot more energy and nutrients for their body size than adults. But as obesity among children in this age group increases in the UK, it is important to limit high-fat and sugary foods and drinks. To grow, keep healthy and fight off illnesses, children need a healthy balanced diet.

Protein foods – to build muscle. Give them moderate amounts of lean meat, chicken, fish, eggs, beans and lentils.

Complex carbohydrates – for energy. Give them plenty of starchy foods such as bread, pasta and rice. Don't worry too much about going totally wholemeal when your children are young, as a diet that is too high in fibre can fill children up too quickly, so that they don't eat enough to obtain the vitamins and minerals they need. Older children, however, can benefit from a higher fibre diet.

Dairy products – for calcium, used to build healthy bones. Don't give children skimmed milk until they're at least five years old because it's too low in calories, and very low in vitamins A and D, which are important for growing children.

Healthy fats – for energy, and their skin and nervous system. Although you should watch children's total fat intake, to help them avoid putting on excess weight, children should still have some of the monounsaturated and polyunsaturated fats that we all need. You'll find these healthy fats in oily fish, nuts and seeds, and nut and seed oils, such as sunflower oil and sunflower spread. Like adults, children over the age of five should eat two portions of oily fish a week.

Fruit and vegetables – like all of us, children should eat at least five portions of fruit and vegetables a day, to supply vitamins, minerals, phytochemicals and fibre.

WATCH OUT!

An alarming number of children could be storing up health problems for the future. An early diet high in fat, sugar and salt can lead to 'adult' symptoms such as raised blood pressure, being seen in children.

A child eating a junk-food diet is taking their first steps on the long road that can lead to obesity, heart disease, diabetes or stroke. But if you can head your child off onto the right track, you can set in motion a healthy eating pattern for life.

Fat: Watch your child's intake of saturated and trans fats (hydrogenated and partially-hydrogenated fats) – many processed foods are worryingly high in these. Saturated fats are also found in animal products – by choosing lean meat and low-fat dairy products, you gain the benefits of the protein, vitamins and minerals in the food, while reducing the fat content. Vegetarian protein sources such as beans and lentils have the benefit of the protein without the saturated fat.

Sugar: So many of the foods targeted at children are smothered with sugar. If children fill up with sugary foods, they're less likely to want proper nutritious meals, which could lead to them missing out on vital nutrients. And many foods with added sugar are high in calories, so could contribute to excess weight gain.

Sugar also contributes to tooth decay, especially when consumed between meals. Try to cut your children's intake of sweets and confectionary, fizzy drinks and squash, to a minimum, and only as part of a meal.

Salt: Children eating a lot of processed and fast food could well be eating too much salt. The recommended maximum for adults is 6g per day, but the amount for children is less, because of their smaller size. And too much salt can contribute to high blood pressure – an important factor in heart disease and stroke.

Recommended maximums of salt and sodium for children – less is better		
Age	Salt per day	Sodium per day
4 – 6 years	Max 3g	Max 1.2g
7 – 10 years	Max 5g	Max 2g
11 and over	Max 6g	Max 2.5g

TEENAGERS

Teenagers can put away a huge amount of food! This is the stage when their nutrient demands are at their greatest, but unfortunately, the teenage years are when many young people's diets go off the rails, as they are bombarded with advertising for fatty, sugary foods, they want to fit in with their friends, and may not think it looks 'cool' to eat healthily.

But what's so cool about gorging on chips and pizza, and glugging back gallons of fizzy drink, if it's going to make you fat, lethargic and unhealthy? Isn't it more attractive to be fit and healthy, with clear skin, lustrous hair and bags of energy?

Parents and the adults they live with are the most important influences on a child's life. Your attitudes to what you eat and drink will directly influence what they choose to eat. If you have a healthy attitude towards food and demonstrate good eating habits yourself, they are more likely to follow your example. But if you adopt a 'do as I say, not as I do' attitude and feed your children healthily, while snacking on junk food yourself, they may become confused and resentful.

Eating healthily is a lesson children have to be taught. But it won't always be easy to achieve and it's important not to take the fun out of eating.

Offer children a variety of fruit and vegetables, fresh meals including protein and complex carbohydrates (starchy foods like bread, pasta and rice), and healthy snacks. Childhood is when most of our food preferences are formed, and younger children are more receptive to new tastes than older ones – so start them young, by offering fun, child-sized portions of healthy foods.

Key nutrients for kids:

Iron – for growth. Iron is needed to build muscle and red blood cells, and prevent anaemia. Teenage girls need to ensure a good source of this mineral, because they lose iron every month once their periods start.

Best food sources: Red meat. Vegetarian sources include dried fruit, beans and lentils, and green leafy vegetables.

Calcium – for building healthy bones. It's important to build up as much bone mass as possible in adolescence and young adulthood, to lessen the risk of the bone-thinning disease, osteoporosis, later in life. Adequate calcium is particularly important for teenage girls, because women are at higher risk of osteoporosis.

Best food sources: Low-fat dairy products. Vegetarian sources include tofu, and soya milk fortified with calcium.

Vitamin D – also needed for healthy bones.

Best sources: The effect of sunlight on the skin (but ensure that children are protected from strong sun). Food sources include oily fish, and spreads.

Vitamin C – for the immune system. It also enhances the absorption of vital iron.

Best food sources: fruit and vegetables.

Folate/folic acid – for the immune system. An increased intake is advised for girls once they reach child-bearing age.

Best food sources: green vegetables, brown rice, wholegrains.

Fizzy Drinks and Bones

There is some evidence that drinks containing caffeine, such as cola and some other fizzy drinks (and also coffee), can cause excess excretion of calcium from the body. Also, the phosphoric acid in some fizzy drinks can hinder calcium uptake from food. It therefore makes sense to avoid fizzy drinks, or at least minimise our intake of them. This is especially important for children and teenagers, as this is the time to build up strong bones and maximise bone density.

What is a child-sized portion?

A portion is roughly the amount of a fruit or vegetable that the child can hold in his or her cupped hands, so the portion grows as the child does.

The portions could be derived from choosing five of the following:

Fruit

◆ A small apple, banana or pear
◆ A dozen grapes
◆ A kiwi fruit or plum
◆ 6–8 small strawberries
◆ 2–3 tablespoons of tinned fruit
◆ A satsuma or clementine

Vegetables

◆ 2 broccoli spears
◆ 3–4 cherry tomatoes
◆ A carrot (cooked or raw)
◆ 6–8 sticks of raw vegetable
◆ 6–8 cucumber slices
◆ 2 tablespoons of peas, sweet corn or other cooked vegetable

And here are some less obvious ways of working towards your five-a-day:

◆ You can count one glass of fruit juice (but only one) towards your target.
◆ One small tin of baked beans in tomato sauce counts too – because of the tomato! Be sure to choose the no-sugar version.
◆ A portion (½–1 tbsp) of dried fruit, such as figs, apricots, raisins or sultanas, counts towards your quota too.

Try to limit the amount of processed food they eat, as this is often very high in fat, salt or sugar, as well as additives. But remember it never pays to ban less healthy foods completely and the occasional treats will do no harm. Help them to develop a taste for savoury foods by giving them new foods to try, and encourage them to drink water and low-sugar drinks.

FIVE-A-DAY

Children, like adults, should be eating at least five portions of fruit and vegetables a day but we know that for many youngsters, achieving it is easier said than done.

The five-a-day message is failing badly where children are concerned and it's important to try to persuade them to eat more. Research has shown that children eat less than half the recommended amount despite 'free fruit in school' programmes, healthy eating lessons and tasting sessions.

Try giving your child fruit as snacks between meals. Cut up a couple of pieces of fruit and arrange them on a plate to make it something a bit special, or put some berry fruits or cherries into a bowl. Have them ready when the children come home from school. They are usually hungry then and before you know it, that can be two of the daily portions eaten.

Here are some other ideas:

● Include small salad leaves and vegetable sticks (carrots, celery, pepper and cucumber) in their lunchboxes
● Add some banana slices or dried fruit to their breakfast cereal
● Try to make sure that your dessert includes fresh or tinned fruit, with perhaps some yogurt or fromage frais
● Raisins, sultanas and dried apricots are popular with children – have a bowl in the kitchen that they can dip into. They are also good as school-time snacks
● Eat plenty of fruit and vegetables yourself. Children are more likely to eat them if they see that you enjoy them

FEEDING FUSSY EATERS

Most children go through a fussy-eating phase at some stage of their growing up. But it's worth trying to tackle the issue early, without letting it get out of proportion, or turning into a confrontation.

Build up their appetites by making sure that they get plenty of fresh air and exercise and limit snacks to two healthy ones each day. This way they will come to the table hungry.

Let them serve their own food onto their plates so that they make their own choices. Introduce new foods to all of the family to show children that it is exciting to discover new tastes, textures and flavours. Try to serve children the same food as the adults.

ACTION
KEEPING CHILDREN ACTIVE

Healthy eating is only part of the way to a healthy lifestyle for children, as it is for adults. Exercise forms the rest of the equation.

We've all read reports of Britain's children becoming a nation of little couch potatoes, slumped watching the television or spending hours in front of the computer screen. A recent survey revealed that only half of all children get the minimum of one hour's exercise at least five days a week.

When it comes to exercise for children it needs to be fun, but it doesn't have to be expensive. There are many activities that can involve the whole family. Walking, cycling, swimming, taking the dog for a walk, or just kicking a ball around together in the park are ideal activities for everyone. Children often copy their parents' behaviour, so it's a good idea to find activities you can all participate in. Many adult sports clubs also have junior sections.

Encourage your children to enjoy sports – it's just a matter of seeing what's available in your area, and letting your child pick a sport that suits their personality. Other ideas:

- Have some play equipment at home so that they can get some exercise without really thinking about it. Have a spacehopper, balls, a trampoline, basketball rings, and skipping ropes.
- Walk to school with them – the exercise will do you both good. Or if the journey is too far and you generally take the car, don't go right to the school, but park a distance away and walk the last part together.
- Cut down the amount of time spent watching television and on the computer. Agree television and computer times and stick to them.

Taking part in regular physical activity increases a child's self-esteem, and can also help reduce the risk of obesity-related problems like cardiovascular disease and diabetes in later life. Weight-bearing exercise also strengthens the bones, helping to prevent osteoporosis.

Remember that active children need plenty of water to keep them hydrated.

Exercise for children

Some children love being part of a team, and would probably enjoy:
Football
Rugby
Hockey
Cricket
Netball

If they prefer to compete as an individual, how about:
Gymnastics
Tennis
Squash
Badminton
Athletics
Archery

Or if they're not the competitive type, then how about:
Dance classes
Roller skating
Ice skating
Junior yoga

Sports classes are often available at leisure centres after school and at weekends.

Jenny and Jason Betts

Jenny Betts, 40, and her 18-year-old son Jason together weighed an enormous 31 stone. Jason's problem was his sweet tooth. He often drank 70 teaspoons of sugar a week in his cups of tea alone, equivalent to 35 jam filled doughnuts. Jenny, who felt older than her 40 years, tended to comfort eat. She had an unhealthy liking for pork pie and pickle sandwiches.

When presented with Jason's food intake for one week, both mother and son were shocked by how much fat they saw. Jenny became tearful when Gillian told her that she was responsible for her son's weight problem as well as her own, and the pair resolved to make big changes to improve their health.

Gillian gave Jason and Jenny a holistic once over, looking for signs of deficiencies or health problems. Jenny told Gillian that she had high blood pressure. Looking at Jason's skin, Gillian noticed his spots and said this could be due to a lack of vitamin C in his diet.

Dr Sanjiv Patel analysed Jenny and Jason's blood samples in the lab. The results revealed that Jason was indeed deficient in vitamin C, and Gillian prescribed a diet rich in leafy green vegetables, blackcurrants and berries to combat the problem.

Once the Betts had consulted their GP, Gillian introduced them to the foods that would make up their new way of life, including fresh greens, fruit and pulses. Jason tried his new breakfast – a raspberry smoothie rich in vitamin C, good for collagen in the skin – and Jenny, who hated celery, promised to drink celery and parsley juice for the health benefits.

By week four the Betts had devised a timetable with Gillian to ensure the work was divided fairly between them, and they started to enjoy walks together and visits to the gym for light exercise. Both already felt more confident and found healthy alternatives to evenings in front of television eating take away food.

After eight weeks the new Jenny and Jason looked fantastic. They had each lost over 2 stone and vowed to continue to eat healthily. Jenny's whole attitude towards food and shopping had changed and Gillian was delighted to hear that Jenny's blood pressure had dropped 30 points and was continuing to decrease. Jason's spots were clearing up and they both had much more energy than before. A coy Jenny admitted to going on a date, the first in a while, and Jason commented that his self-esteem had improved no end.

MENU PLANNER
OCTOBER IDEAS

OCTOBER BEST BUYS

Make the most of:

Apples

Elderberries

Squash

Beetroot

Mushrooms

Courgette

Marrow

Kale

Menu 1

 **Breakfast** — Orange and raisin wholemeal drop scones

Lunch — Home-made chicken nuggets

 Dinner — Spaghetti squash with chunky tomato sauce

Fragrant creamy rice pudding with dried fruit

Menu 2

 Breakfast — Banana, mango and peach smoothie

Lunch — Veggie cakes with sweet corn and pepper salsa

Dinner — Shake and bake honey soy drumsticks

Warmed spiced fruit salad

Menu 1
☼ Orange and raisin wholemeal drop scones

100g wholemeal self-raising flour

2tsp caster sugar

¼ tsp baking powder

Finely grated juice and zest of ½ an orange

1 medium egg

50g sultanas

150ml skimmed milk

1tsp olive oil

1 tin mandarin oranges in juice

Low-fat fromage frais to serve

Makes 12, serves 4

1 Drain the mandarin oranges and set aside.
2 Sift the flour into a mixing bowl (do not discard the tiny flakes that remain, add these to the bowl). Stir in the sugar and baking powder. Add the orange zest and the sultanas.
3 Gradually beat in the egg and milk to make a smooth batter. Add the orange juice.
4 Wipe a large flat-based griddle pan or frying pan with a little olive oil and heat.
5 Using a tablespoon, drop small rounds of the mixture onto the pan.
6 Cook until small bubbles appear on the top surface. Carefully turn the drop scones over and cook for a further 2 minutes. Place on a plate and keep warm. Repeat until all of the mixture is used.
7 Place a stack of 3 pancakes on each plate. Serve with mandarin orange segments and a tablespoon of fromage frais or low-fat set yogurt.

☼ Home-made chicken nuggets

Sunflower oil, for greasing

2 medium slices wholegrain or wholemeal bread, made into fresh breadcrumbs

1 medium free-range egg, beaten

2 boneless, skinless free-range chicken breasts, each about 140g

Freshly cooked seasonal vegetables or a large salad

Serves 4–6 children (makes about 20 nuggets)

1 Preheat the oven to 200°C/Gas 6. Lightly oil a nonstick baking tray. Divide the breadcrumbs between 2 cereal bowls. Place the beaten egg in a third bowl. Cut each chicken breast into 8–10 bite-sized pieces.
2 Dip the chicken pieces, one at a time, into the beaten egg, then coat evenly in the breadcrumbs. Place on the baking tray. Use one bowl of breadcrumbs at a time and change to the second bowl when the crumbs become too sticky to use effectively.
3 Bake the chicken nuggets for 16–18 minutes until pale golden brown and cooked through. Carefully remove from the oven and turn halfway through the cooking time. Serve with lots of lightly cooked vegetables or a large salad.

Spaghetti squash with chunky tomato sauce

1. Put the squash halves in a large frying pan or flameproof casserole. Pour in enough boiling water to come 2.5cm up the sides of the squash halves. Return the water to the boil, then reduce the heat to low, cover and leave the squash to simmer for 35–40 minutes until tender when pierced with a fork.
2. Meanwhile, heat the oil in a large saucepan, ideally nonstick, over a medium-high heat. Add the onions and stir for 2 minutes. Add the garlic and mushrooms and continue stirring until the onions are soft and just starting to turn golden.
3. Stir in the tomato purée, herbs, sugar and pepper to taste. Add the tomatoes with their juice, carrots and the vegetable stock and bring to the boil. Reduce the heat, half-cover the pan and leave to simmer for 10–15 minutes until thickened. Taste and adjust the seasoning, if necessary.
4. When the squash is tender, use tongs or 2 large forks to lift the halves out of the water. Use a table fork to scrape the flesh lengthways, which will separate into long, spaghetti-like strands. Transfer the squash strands to a platter, top with the mushroom and tomato sauce and sprinkle with parsley. Sprinkle Parmesan cheese over each portion if liked.

1 spaghetti squash, about 1kg, cut in half lengthways with fibres and seeds discarded

Boiling water

1½ tbsp sunflower oil

2 large onions, peeled and chopped

1 large garlic clove, crushed

400g button mushrooms, wiped and quartered

2 medium carrots, peeled and finely diced

1tbsp tomato purée

1tsp dried mixed herbs

Pinch sugar

1 can (400g) chopped tomatoes

250ml ready-made vegetable stock

Salt and freshly ground black pepper

Chopped fresh parsley, to garnish

Freshly grated Parmesan cheese, to serve (optional)

Serves 4

Fragrant creamy rice pudding with dried fruit

350ml water

155g short-grain pudding rice

Pinch of salt

1½ tsp cornflour

400ml skimmed milk

85g 'ready to eat' dried cherries

85g 'ready to eat' dried blueberries

2tbsp caster sugar

2 green cardamom pods, lightly crushed

Finely grated rind of 1 orange

Toasted flaked almonds, to decorate

Serves 4

1 Put the water in a saucepan over a high heat and bring to a boil. Stir in the rice and salt, reduce the heat to low, cover and simmer for about 5 minutes until most of the liquid is absorbed and the surface is dotted with indentations.

2 Meanwhile, put the cornflour in a small bowl and stir in 2 tablespoons of the milk until smooth. Uncover the pan with the rice, pour in the remaining milk and the cornflour mixture; stir for 8–10 minutes or until half the liquid is absorbed.

3 Stir in the cherries, blueberries, sugar, cardamom pods and orange rind and continue stirring until the rice is soft and only a thin layer of liquid remains. Use a spoon to remove the cardamom pods.

4 Spoon into bowls and sprinkle with flaked almonds to serve warm, or cover and leave to cool completely and chill.

Rice provides energy in the form of complex carbohydrate, while the milk is a good source of calcium, needed for healthy bones and teeth. The natural sweetness of the dried fruit means that you don't need so much added sugar.

Menu 2
☀ Banana, mango and peach smoothie

1 Peel the mango, remove the fruit and roughly chop. Wash the peaches. Remove the stones and chop the flesh. Chop the banana into 3 pieces.
2 Place all of the fruit into a blender and whiz until smooth.
3 Add the seeds and yogurt and whiz again for a few seconds until frothy.
4 Pour into glasses and chill.

> **Health fact:** Bananas contain a wealth of minerals – they're a useful source of potassium, zinc, iron and calcium, as well as folic acid.

1 banana

1 mango

2 peaches

300g low-fat yogurt

200ml semi-skimmed milk or calcium-enriched soya milk

2tbsp seeds (e.g. sunflower, pumpkin and sesame), chopped

Serves 4

☀ Veggie cakes with sweet corn and pepper salsa

1 Bring a large pan half-filled with water to the boil. Peel the potatoes and cut into rough 4cm pieces. Add to the water and return to the boil. Cook for 18–20 minutes until very tender.
2 Drain well in a colander then return to the pan. Mash using a potato masher until smooth. Leave to cool for 30 minutes.
3 Weigh the frozen vegetables. Transfer into a saucepan or steamer and cook for 3–5 minutes until tender. Preheat the oven to 220°C/Gas 7. Lightly oil a nonstick baking tray.
3 Beat the mayonnaise into the mashed potato, and add the mixed vegetables, spring onions, and plenty of ground black pepper. Stir together well. Using clean hands, roll the mixture into 16 small balls and place on the baking tray.
4 Press lightly with fingertips to flatten slightly. Bake for 7 minutes then carefully remove from the oven and turn over using a spatula. Return to the oven for a further 7 minutes until golden brown on both sides.
5 Serve with a large, lightly dressed salad or freshly cooked seasonal vegetables.

650g potatoes, preferably Maris Piper

Sunflower oil for greasing

1tbsp low-fat mayonnaise

150g frozen mixed vegetables (peas, carrots and sweet corn)

3 spring onions, trimmed and finely chopped

Freshly ground black pepper

Large lightly dressed salad or freshly cooked seasonal vegetables, to serve

Makes 16, serves 4

☽ Shake and bake honey soy drumsticks

4 large chicken drumsticks

2tbsp tomato puree

2tbsp soy sauce

2tsp runny honey

1tbsp sunflower oil

1tbsp orange juice

Steamed vegetables, to serve

Serves 4

1 Slash the skin of the chicken 2 or 3 times with the tip of a sharp knife. Open a medium-sized food bag and push into a jug, folding down the sides. Spoon in the tomato puree, soy, honey, oil and juice, then pop in the chicken.

2 Twist the bag and tie well, then rub the marinade into the drumsticks. Leave in the fridge for half an hour.

3 Preheat the oven to 180°C/Gas 4. Remove the drumsticks from the bag onto a small ovenproof dish and bake for 20 minutes or until cooked. Check by inserting a sharp knife into the flesh. The juices should run clear. Remove and allow to stand for at least 10 minutes before serving with steamed vegetables.

TIP

● This meal is great cooled and packed in a lunch box.

Chicken is rich in protein, which is needed for growth and repair, and low in fat. It's not as rich in iron as red meat, but it does contain some, and the vitamin C in the tomatoes helps this to be absorbed.

Warmed spiced fruit salad

1 Place the pears, apples and blackberries in an 850ml pie dish in the top of a steamer and sprinkle with the cinnamon.

2 Toss the fruit lightly to coat in the spice. Put the lid on top and steam for 25–30 minutes until all the fruit is very tender.

3 While the fruit is cooking, tip the almonds into a small pan and cook over a medium heat for about a minute until lightly toasted, stirring constantly. Remove from the heat and toss with the sugar.

4 Spoon the warm fruit into dessert bowls and top with the almonds. Serve with spoonfuls of fat-free bio-yogurt, fromage frais or single cream, if liked.

2 pears, peeled, quartered, cored and thickly sliced

2 apples, peeled, quartered, cored and thickly sliced

150g blackberries

½ tsp ground cinnamon

25g flaked almonds

2tsp unrefined demerara sugar

Fat-free bio-yogurt, fromage frais or single cream, to serve

Serves 4

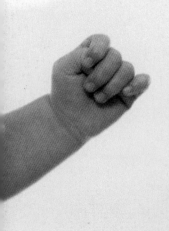

november

THEY ARE WHAT YOU EAT
You know that you are what you eat –
but you're also what your mum ate!
The food eaten during pregnancy has
an enormous effect on a baby's
development, both in the womb and
also after birth.

A mother's diet even affects her baby's health in adulthood – poor maternal nutrition can increase the risk of diseases such as high blood pressure, stroke, heart disease and diabetes when her baby grows up, while a healthy diet in pregnancy gives the baby the best possible start in life.

Pregnant women should always consult their GP on matters of wellbeing and nutrition.

PLANNING A BABY

A woman's diet impacts upon her baby's health even before conception. Good nutrition prepares her body for motherhood, building up her stores of vital nutrients that may become depleted during pregnancy. If she is well nourished at the outset, her body will be able to cope with the demands of pregnancy with only minimal changes to her diet. But if her body is poorly nourished, she'll be more at risk from problems such as anaemia, and her baby may find it harder to obtain the nutrients necessary for development.

Ideally, she should be as near as possible to her ideal weight, and eating really healthily for a good three months before her baby is conceived. The first few weeks of pregnancy, before a woman even knows it's a reality, are the time when the baby's nutrition is most crucial, and deficiencies have the most far-reaching effects on her offspring's health. See later in this chapter for the nutrients that are particularly important for a baby's development.

Poor nutrition at any stage of pregnancy can harm the embryo's development, but problems early on have wider-reaching effects.

The developing baby obtains all of its nutritional need from its mother, which increases her own requirements for many nutrients. The mother's body adapts to this difficult task by becoming super-efficient at absorbing nutrients from her food. Despite the baby's increased demands, if she is eating healthily, her enhanced absorption generally provides all that is needed.

And it's not just about the baby not getting enough nutrients. The baby may also take up substances harmful to its development, such as caffeine and alcohol.

YOU DON'T HAVE TO EAT FOR TWO

Expectant mums need to eat enough to ensure that their baby has all the nutrients it needs to grow, but they certainly don't need to eat for two, at least not as far as calories are concerned. Although a pregnant woman has up to twice the vitamin and mineral needs she had before, she doesn't need any extra calories during the first six months of pregnancy, and only 200 extra calories daily for the final three months.

A good way of obtaining the extra calories is to simply eat an extra serving of complex carbohydrate, such as a slice of wholemeal toast or a jacket potato, plus a small serving of protein, like an ounce of cheese, a glass of skimmed milk or a

It matters for men too!

It takes three months for a man's body to make sperm, so it's a good idea for men to make a special point of eating nutritious food in the months when they and their partner are planning a pregnancy.

A man's baby-making diet should concentrate on boosting his intake of:

◆ Vitamin C – this antioxidant vitamin can help prevent damaged sperm. Particularly rich sources include fruits such as kiwi fruit, strawberries, blackberries and citrus fruit.

◆ Zinc – even a slight zinc deficiency can reduce fertility. Good sources include meat, chicken (especially the dark meat), beans, pumpkin seeds and sunflower seeds.

◆ Calcium and vitamin D – research suggests that getting enough of these nutrients could be important for male fertility.

Men should also:

◆ Make sure that they're as close as possible to their ideal weight.

◆ Cut alcohol down or out.

◆ Cut down on caffeine – found mainly in coffee, tea and energy drinks.

◆ Stop smoking – this is even more vital for mums-to-be

low-fat yogurt. Pregnant women should also maximise their intake of fruit and vegetables (especially dark-green vegetables and citrus fruits) but these will have a negligible impact on their calorie count, provided no fat or sugar is added.

SOME NUTRIENTS ARE PARTICULARLY IMPORTANT DURING PREGNANCY

Vitamin A

Although it's important for expectant mothers to eat enough vitamin A, too much can cause birth defects. To avoid overdosing, pregnant women should not take vitamin A supplements, or eat liver and liver products (such as pâté), since these contain very high levels of vitamin A. They should also avoid fish-liver-oil supplements. However, with a normal, healthy diet, dangerous mega-doses of vitamin A are hard to achieve.

Find vitamin A in good (but not overly rich) dietary sources, such as oily fish, eggs, carrots, red peppers, spinach, broccoli and tomatoes.

Folic acid

For at least four weeks before conception and the first twelve weeks of pregnancy, women should take a supplement of 400 micrograms of folic acid, to reduce the risk of giving birth to a baby with a neural tube defect (NTD) such as spina bifida.

Women who have previously given birth to a baby with a NTD will need a supplement of 4 milligrams of folic acid per day – that's ten times the normal recommendation.

Iron

Babies need good iron stores for the first six months of life, because milk is very low in iron. During pregnancy, the baby builds up its own iron reserve by drawing on its mother's stores of this mineral.

Building the baby's tissues and red blood cells in the womb requires iron too. And the baby is particularly good at ensuring its own supply, even at the expense of its mother's iron stores.

This means that adequate iron is important for expectant mothers. It's possible to achieve this through a healthy diet, but if a woman's iron reserves were low before pregnancy, and fall further as the baby draws on them, her GP or midwife may advise her to take a supplement.

Tip:
Eating vitamin-C-rich foods with iron-rich foods increases absorption of the valuable iron. But coffee and tea decrease iron absorption, so avoid them at mealtimes.

PREGNANCY NUTRIENT CHECKLIST

Nutrient	Why it's needed	Where to find it	Need to know
Essential fatty acids (EFAs)	Important for development of baby's brain and vision	Oily fish, flaxseed (linseed) and flaxseed oil	EFAs from fish oil are easier to absorb than those from vegetarian sources
Calcium	For building baby's bones, and preventing bone mineral loss in the mother	Low-fat dairy products, canned sardines and salmon (eaten with the bones), dried fruit, green leafy vegetables	Vegans need to take extra care regarding their calcium intakes, as vegan foods are generally calcium-poor
Iron	For making red blood cells for the baby, and preventing anaemia in the mother	Red meat (but not liver), beans and lentils, dried fruit, green vegetables	Maximising iron absorption is particularly important for vegetarians, as it's harder for the body to absorb iron from non-animal sources
Zinc	Building baby's cells and supporting the mother's immune system	Meat, fish, chicken, eggs and dairy products – vegan sources include bread and cereals, green leafy vegetables	Zinc from animal products are easiest for the body to use
Folate (the natural form of folic acid, found in food)	Important to help prevent neural tube defects such as spina bifida in the baby	Fruit, dark-green leafy vegetables, brown rice and wholegrains – plus take a folic acid supplement	Folic acid supplements can also help prevent low birth weight
B-vitamins	For building new cells, and energy release	Low-fat milk and other low-fat dairy products, meat, bread and cereals, yeast extract	Getting enough Vitamin B12 is difficult for vegans, who will probably need to take supplements
Vitamin C	Replenishing the mother's vitamin C levels and supporting her immune system, and also helps absorption of iron	Blackcurrants, strawberries, kiwi fruits, citrus fruits, peppers, green vegetables	Cook vegetables lightly, to avoid vitamin C loss
Vitamin D	Important for building healthy bones for the baby	Mainly the effect of sunlight on the skin – dietary sources include spreads, eggs, oily fish	Women with dark skin, or who rarely get out in the sun, and vegans, may need a supplement
Fibre	Preventing constipation	Wholegrains, beans and lentils, fruit and vegetables	Most of the fibre in fruit and vegetables is found in the skin, so scrub thoroughly rather than peeling

WATCH OUT FOR THESE FOODS
Alcohol

Women should cut out alcohol or limit it to certainly no more than one or two drinks, once or twice a week, when pregnant or planning a baby. Alcohol can cause birth defects, particularly during the first few weeks after conception.

Caffeine

High intakes of caffeine can harm the developing baby. If you can't bear to cut out caffeine completely, limit it to no more than 300mg per day. That's the equivalent of two cups of brewed coffee or mugs of instant coffee, plus two cups of tea or cans of cola, but the lower you can go, the better. And remember that caffeine is also found in energy drinks, chocolate (especially dark chocolate) and some painkillers and cold and flu remedies.

Junk food

If you're pregnant or planning a baby, you should try to avoid foods high in fat and sugar, such as cakes, biscuits and sweets. You really need to be maximising your intake of good, nutritious wholefoods, rather than eating harmful processed and saturated fats and empty calories from sugar.

FOODS TO AVOID DURING PREGNANCY

- Blue-veined cheeses, and soft, rind-ripened cheeses like Camembert, Brie or Chevre. Hard cheeses (eg Cheddar), and cottage cheese are fine.
- All kinds of pate (including vegetable).
- Unpasteurised milk. This, and the cheeses and pate mentioned above, can contain Listeria, a germ that is implicated in miscarriage, stillbirth and serious illness in newborn babies.
- Raw or lightly-cooked eggs, to avoid the risk of Salmonella. Eggs should be cooked until the white and yolk are set.
- Avoid swordfish, shark and marlin totally, and don't eat more than two tuna steaks or four small tins a week. These fish can contain mercury, which at high levels could harm your baby's developing nervous system.
- Limit your intake of other oily fish (eg salmon, trout, sardines and mackerel) to no more than twice weekly, because these fish can contain chemical pollutants that could harm your baby at high doses.
- Make sure you don't get too much vitamin A – avoid overly rich sources such as liver and liver products, vitamin A supplements and some multivitamins, and fish liver oil.
- Undercooked meat – be particularly careful with mince.
- Make sure your shellfish is well-cooked, and avoid raw shellfish (such as oysters). Undercooked meat and shellfish should be avoided to minimise the risk of food poisoning bugs that could harm your baby.

Scientists have discovered that by increasing their omega-3 intakes, pregnant women increased their babies' scores in intelligence and perception tests.

Pregnancy is not the time to embark on a weight-loss diet, unless advised to do so by your doctor.

Morning sickness

Morning sickness affects around seventy per cent of women, but there are ways of minimising the nausea and dizziness it causes.

◆ Ginger – try ginger tea, made from grated fresh root ginger steeped in boiling water. Sweeten with a little honey if you need to.

◆ Little and often – avoid that feeling of an overfull stomach, and eat small, frequent meals.

◆ Scent off – strong food smells, such as coffee, vinegar and curries, can trigger nausea in pregnancy. Stay away from places where they're eaten if you find they're triggers for you.

◆ Be good to yourself – if you're well nourished, well rested, and unstressed, you'll be better able to cope.

✔ THIS MONTH, MAKE SURE YOU:

● Eat 5-a-day – eat five portions of fruit and vegetables

● Cut down on caffeine – too much can harm an unborn baby, and excessive caffeine isn't a good idea for anyone

PREGNANCY SUPPLEMENTS

In an ideal world, we'd get all the nutrients we require from healthy, balanced diets. But, especially with the additional demands the baby's development places on an expectant mother's body, pregnancy is a time when you really do need to take a dietary supplement. In fact, it's essential in order to obtain the recommended amount of folic acid.

There are several supplements available that are tailored especially for the pregnant woman's nutritional needs. They contain the recommended extra folic acid, along with other important vitamins and minerals such as vitamins E, C and D, and zinc and calcium.

If you're taking a multivitamin already, you must take qualified nutritional advice before taking any other supplements, and avoid supplements containing vitamin A or retinol (a form of vitamin A), or fish-liver oil (which is very rich in vitamin A).

EXERCISE IN PREGNANCY

Staying active will help keep an expectant mum's body strong, fit and supple, and help prevent many of the symptoms associated with pregnancy, such as constipation and other digestive problems, backache and aching joints, and circulation problems. You just need to be careful about the amount and type of activity you do.

These activities are excellent:

● Swimming – gentle and effective, as the water supports your body. Make sure the water isn't too warm – stick to between 18 and 25 degrees Celsius.

● Walking – as brisk as you feel comfortable with.

Avoid:

● Steam rooms and hot tubs, or exercising in hot, humid weather.

● Sports such as squash, basketball and football, where you might collide with another player.

● Sports involving jerky, bouncy movements, or exercises that involve lying on your back after the first trimester.

● Any sport where you might fall and hurt your baby.

If in doubt whether an activity is safe for you, or if at any stage you experience discomfort during exercise, you should stop immediately and contact your doctor or midwife.

ACTION
MEDITATION AND RELAXATION

We cannot treat our bodies as machines and expect them to thrive. Even if we give our bodies the most nutritious foods, and keep our heart, lungs, bones and muscles in shape with exercise, we still won't function at our best if we don't include our minds.

When we consider total wellbeing, the mind is crucial. And like the body, it needs nourishment, mental exercise – and rest.

How do you relax? Perhaps you phone a friend for a good old gossip? Go bowling, or to see a movie? Play a musical instrument, or read a book?

While all of these may feel 'relaxing' – after all, you're not working – they all stimulate your mind, so your poor brain isn't getting a rest.

What you need is *true* relaxation.

MEDITATION

Don't be scared of meditation. It isn't all about sitting in the lotus position and chanting strange, Eastern mantras. It can be, but alternatively meditation can be anything that you like.

Just ten to twenty minutes each day can make you feel so much calmer. All you need to do is find a quiet place where you won't be disturbed, settle down comfortably in a sitting or lying position, and try to completely empty your mind. Thoughts will keep trying to push their way in – you just need to ignore them. Easier said than done, but if you have something else to focus on, that doesn't involve 'thinking', it's much easier. Here are just a few ideas:

- A candle flame
- A picture
- A beautiful object, such as a flower or ornament
- Concentrating on your breathing
- Chanting a mantra

Unfocus your eyes and gaze at your object, concentrate on breathing slowly in and out, or repeat your mantra. Your mantra can be any word you like the sound of, though many people choose one like peace, calm or love. But you're not supposed to be thinking about its meaning, it's just a sound to focus on to block out the worries of modern life.

Other relaxation techniques

Deep breathing
When we're under stress, our breathing speeds up. Stop, relax, and take ten deep, slow breaths, in through the nose and out through the mouth.

Relax your muscles
We often tense up when stressed. Consciously relax your muscles – the jaw and shoulders are notorious tension traps.

Visualisation
Picture a place where you remember happy, peaceful times. Close your eyes and hold the place in your mind – hear the sounds, smell the scents and watch the scene unfold.

MENU PLANNER
NOVEMBER IDEAS

 **NOVEMBER BEST BUYS**

Make the most of:

Cranberries

Pears

Swede

Leeks

Cabbage

Cauliflower

Broccoli

Brussels sprouts

Potatoes

Parsnips

Chestnuts

Beetroot

Menu 1

Breakfast — Poached eggs with spinach on toast

Lunch — Chunky lentil and vegetable soup

Dinner — One-pan roast chicken and vegetables

Light bread-and-butter pudding

Menu 2

Breakfast — Stewed apple and breakfast loaf

Lunch — Red pepper and sweet potato soup

Dinner — Orange and ginger salmon

Oaty apple crumble

Menu 1
☀ Poached eggs with spinach

1 Fill a medium saucepan with 4cm cold water. Add the vinegar and bring to the boil. Once boiling, remove from the heat. One at a time, break the eggs into a cup, and slip into the water, spacing well apart.
2 Reduce the heat to low and return the pan to the hob. Cook the eggs very gently for about 4 minutes for a softly set yolk or longer if you prefer (loosen with a spoon if the egg white sticks to the bottom of the pan).
3 Meanwhile, heat the oil over a low heat in another pan, add the spinach and cook for about 2 minutes, stirring regularly until wilted.
4 Toast the bread.
5 Put the bread on 4 plates. Season the spinach with freshly ground black pepper and pile onto the toast. Drain the eggs with a slotted spoon and place on top. Serve immediately.

2tsp white wine or cider vinegar

4 very fresh, large free-range eggs (from the fridge)

2tsp sunflower or olive oil

100g baby spinach leaves, washed and drained

4 medium slices wholegrain bread

Freshly ground black pepper

Serves 4

> **Health fact:** Eggs are a source of vitamin D, essential for the absorption of calcium, which is needed for healthy bones. They also provide good amounts of vitamins A, E, B2 and B12. Spinach is rich in betacarotene, as well as providing vitamin C and folate – both can help to keep the heart healthy, and are important in pregnancy.

☼ Chunky lentil and vegetable soup

1tbsp virgin olive oil

2 garlic cloves, peeled and crushed

2 medium onions, peeled and sliced

1tsp (heaped) finely grated root ginger

1tsp hot chilli powder

3 medium carrots, peeled and sliced

2 medium parsnips, peeled and cut into small cubes

1 large sweet potato, peeled and cut into small cubes

175g red split lentils

1 organic vegetable stock cube

1 medium leek, trimmed and sliced

Fresh parsley sprigs, to garnish (optional)

Serves 4–6

1   Heat the oil in a large saucepan or flameproof casserole over a low heat and cook the garlic and onions for 5 minutes until softened but not coloured, stirring occasionally.

2   Add the ginger and chilli powder and cook with the onions for a few seconds before adding the carrots, parsnips and sweet potato. Add the lentils to the pan and stir well. Crumble the stock cube on top and pour over 1.5 litres (2¾ pints) of cold water.

3   Bring to the boil, then reduce the heat and simmer gently for 10 minutes, stirring occasionally. Remove any foam that rises to the surface with a spoon. Add the sliced leek and simmer for a further 8–10 minutes until the lentils are tender.

4   Serve in warmed bowls, garnished with fresh parsley if liked. Alternatively, blend the soup for a smoother texture, then serve topped with spoonfuls of low-fat bio-yogurt and freshly chopped coriander.

TIPS

● This soup will keep well in the fridge for up to two days. Cool, then transfer to a rigid container before chilling. Heat through thoroughly before serving. It also freezes well, but is better blended first.

● You can use any root vegetables you like for this soup, just keep quantities roughly the same and don't be afraid to add extra water if the soup seems too thick.

● If you don't have fresh root ginger handy, just add half a teaspoon of ground ginger instead.

Sweet potatoes contain more vitamin E than any other low-fat food, which together with betacarotene and vitamin C helps fight harmful free radicals in the body.

☾ One-pan roast chicken and vegetables

8 free-range chicken thighs, skinned

1tsp virgin olive oil

2 medium courgettes, trimmed and cut into 1cm slices

1 large sweet potato, peeled and cut into 3cm chunks

1 red pepper, deseeded and cut into 4cm chunks

1 yellow pepper, deseeded and cut into 4cm chunks

1 red onion, peeled and cut into 8–10 wedges

1tbsp chopped fresh rosemary or thyme leaves (optional)

Freshly ground black pepper

Serves 4

1 Preheat the oven to 200°C/Gas 6. Place the chicken in a large roasting tin and brush a little of the oil over each thigh. Sprinkle with the rosemary or thyme and season with ground black pepper. Turn to coat in the oil and seasonings. Bake for 15 minutes.

2 Remove the tin from the oven and carefully add all the vegetables. Turn the vegetables to coat in the cooking juices. Season with black pepper.

3 Return the tin to the oven for a further 30 minutes until the chicken is golden and cooked through (there should be no pink remaining) and the vegetables are tender. Remove the tin from the oven and carefully turn the chicken and vegetables halfway through the cooking time.

Health fact: As well as providing low-fat protein from the chicken, this dish also gives a real antioxidant boost, thanks to the red and yellow peppers and the sweet potato.

Light bread-and-butter pudding

4–6 slices of wholemeal bread

Low-fat spread

25g brown sugar

50g sultanas or raisins

1 medium egg

600ml skimmed milk

Grated nutmeg (optional)

Serves 4–6

1 Lightly grease a 1.2-litre ovenproof dish with low-fat spread.

2 Very thinly spread each slice of bread with low-fat spread and cut into triangles. Place a layer of bread triangles in the bottom of the dish and sprinkle over half of the fruit and sugar. Arrange a second layer of bread triangles in the dish and sprinkle with the remaining sugar and fruit.

3 Beat the egg into the milk and pour through a strainer into the dish. Dust with grated nutmeg, if liked. Cover the dish with foil. Leave the dish to stand for 30 minutes before placing in an oven preheated to 180°C/Gas 4.

4 Bake for 1 hour, then remove the foil and bake for a further 25 minutes, or until the custard is set and the top is golden brown and crisp.

Health fact: The sultanas in this dish supply natural sugars, so you don't need so much added sugar. The milk is an excellent source of calcium, needed for healthy bones at all stages of life.

Menu 2
☼ Stewed apple and breakfast loaf

1. Heat the oven to 160°C/Gas 3. Line a 20x10x5cm loaf tin with nonstick baking paper.
2. Cream the low-fat spread and sugar together until light and fluffy. Fold in the eggs.
3. Weigh out the flour into a bowl and add the figs, apricots and spice. Fold the dry ingredients into the creamed mixture, and spoon into the prepared loaf tin.
4. Bake for an hour or until a skewer inserted into the centre of the loaf comes out clean. Leave to cool and store in an airtight tin.
5. To make the stewed apple, place the chopped apple in a saucepan with the water and a little nutmeg or cinnamon if desired. Boil gently until the apples collapse. Add a little honey, if needed.
6. To serve, place a slice of breakfast loaf on a plate with some stewed apple and a tablespoon of low-fat fromage frais.

> **Health fact:** Apples contain a compound called quercetin, which acts as an antioxidant and may help prevent heart disease and cancer.

TIP
- This delicious high-fibre loaf can also be made in individual muffin cases and baked for 30 minutes. They make a nutritious addition to a lunchbox.

100g low-fat spread (suitable for baking)

50g dark brown sugar

100g dried 'ready to eat' figs, chopped

50g dried 'ready to eat' apricots, chopped

125g wholemeal self-raising flour

1tsp mixed spice or cinnamon

2 medium eggs

Stewed apple (for 4):

450g cooking or tart eating apples, peeled, cored and chopped

5fl.oz water

Nutmeg or cinnamon

Honey to drizzle

Makes 8 slices

☼ Red pepper and sweet potato soup

1 Slice the onion, peppers, sweet potato and carrots. Heat the oil in a large saucepan and gently cook the vegetables with the garlic for 10 minutes until softened, stirring regularly.
2 Crumble the stock cube into the pan and add the water. Bring to the boil, then reduce the heat and simmer for 15–20 minutes until all the vegetables are tender, stirring occasionally. Remove pan from the heat and leave to cool for at least 20 minutes.
3 Add the soup to a food processor or blender, being careful to avoid splashes. Blend until smooth.
4 Return to the pan and heat through gently. Season with a little ground black pepper and ladle into warmed bowls. Garnish with fresh basil leaves.

Health fact: Sweet potatoes contain about fifty times more vitamin E than ordinary white potatoes. Vitamin E helps protect the heart and blood vessels, as well as promoting healthy skin and boosting the immune system.

1 medium onion, peeled and trimmed

2 red peppers, deseeded and quartered

1 medium sweet potato, peeled and quartered lengthways

2 medium carrots, peeled

1tbsp olive oil

1 garlic clove, peeled and sliced

900ml just-boiled water

1 organic vegetable stock cube

Freshly ground black pepper

Fresh basil leaves, to serve

Serves 4

Sweet peppers are a great source of betacarotene (which the body can convert to vitamin A), as are red peppers, which are also an excellent source of vitamin C.

☾ Orange and ginger salmon

4tbsp tamari soy sauce

2 garlic cloves, crushed

2tsp finely grated fresh root ginger

Freshly squeezed juice of 2 oranges

4x125g salmon fillets, skinned

12 spring onions, trimmed

Sunflower oil, for greasing

Serves 4

1 Place the soy sauce, garlic, ginger and orange juice in a bowl and mix well. Add the salmon and turn to coat in the marinade. Cover and leave to marinate in the fridge for 30–60 minutes.

2 Lightly oil and preheat an electric health grill or ridged griddle pan. Lift the salmon out of the marinade and shake off any excess. Place on the grill or griddle. Add the spring onions. Cook for 4–5 minutes, until cooked to taste. If using a health grill, close the lid. If using a griddle, turn the fish over halfway through the cooking time.

3 Remove the salmon and onions from the grill or griddle and stand for 3 minutes before serving.

4 Serve the salmon topped with spring onions and accompanied by freshly steamed or stir-fried vegetables and cooked noodles.

Oaty apple crumble

200g muesli

2tbsp pumpkin seeds

2tbsp sunflower seeds

25g walnuts, chopped

50g sultanas or raisins

2tsp ground cinnamon

1tbsp brown sugar

50g low-fat spread

2 large cooking apples

6tbsp water

Serves 4

1 Preheat the oven to 180°C/Gas 4.Place the muesli, 1tsp of the cinnamon, seeds and nuts into a mixing bowl.

2 Gently melt the low-fat spread in a small saucepan. Add to the dry mixture and combine thoroughly.

3 Peel, core and slice the apples and lay them in a baking dish. Sprinkle over the brown sugar, the raisins or sultanas and the remainder of the cinnamon. Add the water.

4 Spoon the crumble mixture over the apples. Bake in the oven for about 40 minutes. Serve with low-fat yogurt or fromage frais

Health fact: Nuts and seeds are great sources of the 'good' fats, which help keep our hearts healthy. They're also packed with protein.

Salmon is an excellent source of essential omega-3 fatty acids, which help prevent cardio-vascular disease, balance hormones and promote healthy skin. Oranges contain vitamin C, a powerful antioxidant that protects cells from free-radical damage and supports immunity.

december

THE SECRETS OF A HEALTHY FESTIVE SEASON

Most of us would admit that we eat and drink more than we should over the Christmas holiday and compound the assault on our bodies by slumping in front of the television.

- Banish the frying pan – switch to low fat cooking methods
- Eat breakfast – a sustaining breakfast makes it so much easier to stick to your food resolutions

Chocolates

If Christmas isn't Christmas without chocolate, then treat yourself to a small box or bar of connoisseur chocolates made with pure ingredients and without hydrogenated vegetable fat or a whole list of E-numbers, additives and preservatives. Go for chocolate high in cocoa solids – seventy per cent or above is best. The higher the cocoa solids, the less room there is for sugar and fat, and the more intense the chocolaty flavour. Ration your chocolate so that it's all the more special, and enjoy!

Did you know that the average Britain consumes 7,000 calories on Christmas Day alone? But it's not just the Christmas dinner that does the damage, it's all of the other things we eat and drink. It's that box of chocolates, the nibbles with cocktails, and all the alcohol itself.

But somehow it's all part of Christmas and we do it every year . . . until this year, that is. With your new healthy outlook on life, there is a whole world of fresh, healthy dishes you can prepare without taking the tradition out of the festivities or feeling even the teeniest bit hard done by. The secret of a healthy Christmas is in moderation, not self-denial!

If you want to survive the run-up to Christmas with enough energy to enjoy it, the trick is to plan ahead. Vow to keep food simple, making as much use as you can of the seasonal fruit and vegetables, especially the citrus fruits which are so much part of Christmas.

To get you started there are some delicious healthy suggestions in our December menu planner to add to your festive menus, as well as a host of hints for party food and drink, and some good wheezes to help you make healthy choices at parties.

Think ahead

Plan your menus for the holiday. Make lists of what you need to buy, and when. Leave the fresh food as late as you can – but make sure that you have placed any orders you need to. Stock up on store-cupboard items early.

CHRISTMAS DAY
Breakfast

Start your day with a simple, light but sustaining breakfast – you don't want to be diving for the biscuits and chocolates by ten o'clock. Make sure that you include some protein, like yogurt or milk, and some complex, starchy carbohydrate to keep your energy levels up.

Lunch is served

- Prepare as many of the elements of the meal yourself as you can – that way, you control the sugar, fat and salt. If you are planning 'turkey and all the trimmings', there are some easy ways to trim the fat which no one will even notice.
- Roast the turkey on a rack so that the fat can drain off, and remove the skin before serving the meat onto the plates.
- Instead of chipolata sausages wrapped in streaky bacon, wrap ready-to-eat prunes in tiny strips of back bacon. Stretch the bacon rashers using the back of a knife and you'll make them go twice as far.
- Make your own stuffing using brown breadcrumbs, finely chopped onion and fresh herbs, bound together with egg. Avoid adding butter to the stuffing or dotting the top with pieces of butter before putting the stuffing into the oven. Don't be tempted to make the stuffing into balls to fry them.

- Try making your bread sauce with wholemeal breadcrumbs (or half and half).
- If you use pan juices to make the gravy, strain away all of the fat first.
- Sweeten home-made cranberry sauce with honey, and use less sweetening than you normally would.
- Serve just a few roasted potatoes, and more steamed or boiled potatoes.
- Whatever people say about the 'crispiness' it's said to give, don't be tempted to use duck or goose fat to roast your potatoes. A light spray of olive oil is fine, but remember to keep turning them. Do not roast potatoes alongside the turkey, as they will absorb its fat.
- Serve large quantities of freshly cooked vegetables. If you put different vegetables in separate dishes, you will find that people will put more on their plates, as they take some from each.
- If Christmas isn't Christmas without the pudding, have a small piece and forgo the cream and brandy butter in favour of quark flavoured with a little brandy, or a home-made rum sauce.
- Make lidless mince pies with filo pastry, and moisten the leaves of pastry with egg white rather than melted butter. Make your own mincemeat without the suet – it doesn't need it. Simply chop half of the apple called for in the recipe, and stew the other half. This will keep the mincemeat moist while it is cooking.

Supper

- Make supper a simple light meal.
- Cold meats, a colourful array of salads, with salsas and low-fat dressings, are all that is needed to end a perfect day.

PARTY TIME

Christmas parties are another time when we all need to call on our stores of willpower. Enjoy the ambience and the company, and let food and drink play second fiddle.

Some party food can be scarily high in saturated fat, so knowing what to choose from the delicious array of dishes on the buffet table or from the tempting canapés on offer makes good sense.

With so much ready-made party food available in supermarkets at Christmas time, it's hardly surprising that busy hostesses make a dash to stock up their fridges. After all, it's one less thing to worry about. But delicious though it may look, much of it is less than healthy, and a good proportion will have been fried, such as the mini versions of the Indian and Chinese starters we are all familiar with – the bhajis, samosas, pakoras and the prawn toasts and crispy wontons. But there are still some party time-savers that you can pick up from the supermarket, if you read the labels. Opt for soft cheese wrapped in salmon, sushi or low-fat dips that you can serve with crudités, as a standby.

But if you can make time to make some healthy canapés, your guests will be most impressed to be offered something fresh, tasty and, above all, different.

There's so much more to Christmas time than eating and drinking:

- Switch off the telly and play charades, dominoes or pin the tail on the donkey. Get out a board game or a pack of cards.
- Get out the holiday brochures and plan a holiday . . . or just dream.
- Book tickets for a pantomime – the laughing will do you a power of good.
- Take a trip to an ice rink – it's great exercise and fun.
- Wrap up warm, and go for a walk – it'll help burn off those extra Christmas calories.

Natty nibbles

Instead of putting out bowls of crisps and salted peanuts for your guests (and for the family), fill the bowls with mixed nuts, raisins and seeds or pretzels, mini oatcakes, plain popcorn, home-made garlic bagel chips (see page 148) or pesto pitta-bread crisps (see page 217) .

BUFFET SURVIVAL

Knowing what to choose from plates of delicious canapés and nibbles will help you to keep on the healthy straight and narrow.

- Put some food on your plate and move away from the buffet table. Don't stand by the table and pick.
- Avoid anything deep-fried, in a creamy sauce or made with puff pastry.
- Pile your plate high with crudités and salad vegetables – even if they were intended as garnish.
- Don't imagine small is beautiful – one tiny vol-au-vent can pack a hefty fat punch.
- From a cold-meat platter, choose chicken, turkey (remove any skin) or lean ham. Give salami, liver sausage and other processed meats a miss.
- Take a very small portion of creamy pasta dishes or curries and fill the rest of your plate with salad.
- Eat in a well-lit part of the room. Studies have shown that we lose our inhibitions and eat more when the lights are turned down low!

SMART BUFFET SWAPS

Swap...	For a healthier...
Sausage roll	Cocktail sausage
Spring roll	Piece of sushi
Slice of pizza	Tomato-topped bruschetta
Piece of Stilton	Piece of Brie
Bombay mix	Twiglets
Cream cheese dip	Tomato salsa
Prawn crackers	Oatcakes
Vol-au-vents	Chicken strips

Be kind to yourself

If you do fall off the healthy eating wagon over Christmas and the New Year, don't worry about it. You're only human, and it is the season of goodwill, after all. Don't feel guilty. Forgive yourself, and simply start again where you left off.

If you tell yourself you're a failure, and make yourself miserable about your little lapse, you're more likely to slip back onto a downward spiral of unhealthy eating habits in the New Year.

Remember, tomorrow is a new day, next year is a new year, and you've got so much potential. Fulfil it!

HAPPY NEW YEAR!

New Year's parties can be a wobbly time if you're trying to eat healthily – all that freely flowing alcohol and fatty, salty snacks. But with the nutritional nous you've gained from this book, you can make healthy choices – and still have a great time.

And if you're the party host or hostess, there's no excuse not to get your New Year off to a healthy start.

Here are some ideas for quick canapés:

- Make bases for canapés using filo pastry. Cut small triangles of pastry and brush with lightly beaten egg white. Lay three layers of pastry (each one at a 45-degree angle from the one below) in mini muffin cases and bake until golden and crispy. You can also make your own canapé bases by cutting circles from wholemeal bread or bagels and baking them slowly in the oven. Pumpernickel and rye bread also make ideal bases for canapés because they are dense.

- For healthy canapés, add tasty low-fat toppings to small pieces of vegetable. Try small pieces of cucumber with the seeds scooped out, halved cherry tomatoes with the seeds removed, pieces of red pepper, small pieces of celery or halved chicory leaves. Make sure that any filling you make is not too wet.
- Lay a thin slice of lean ham on a board. Combine a little low-fat cheese with a squeeze of ready-made English mustard. Spread on the ham and roll up. Cut the rolls into bite-sized pieces and secure with a cocktail stick. Thin slices of lean roast beef also work well, if you use low-fat soft cheese combined with horseradish sauce.
- Stir-fry strips of chicken with a little soy sauce and chilli. Serve with a low-fat yogurt and mint dip.
- Combine two tablespoons of finely chopped cucumber (seeds and skin removed) with a small tin of red salmon, a tablespoon of low-fat mayonnaise, a pinch of chilli powder and black pepper. Put teaspoons of the mixture on chicory leaves or squares of rye bread.
- Combine low-fat cream cheese with a little drained and finely chopped pineapple and red pepper. Put a small teaspoonful of the mixture on healthy bases such as mini oatcakes, or pieces of vegetable.
- Make mini pizzas. Slice a wholemeal baguette horizontally. Make a quick tomato topping by combining a small tin of tomatoes, a tablespoon of tomato purée, half a teaspoon of dried mixed herbs and a little freshly ground black pepper. Spread the topping on the halves of baguette and top with small pieces of vegetable. Grate over a little half-fat mature cheese or mozzarella. Bake until the bread is crisp and the cheese is melted. Cut the pizza into 2cm strips and serve.

YOU ARE WHAT YOU DRINK

For many of us, the festive season just wouldn't be festive without a drink or two … or three. A glass of brandy by the fireside, cocktails at a party, hot toddies to warm you up after a bracing walk outside, and Champagne to toast the New Year.

After all, a little alcohol is good for you, isn't it? What was that about red wine helping to keep your heart healthy?

The key word is 'little'. While a small glass of red wine every day or two can help prevent heart disease, thanks to the polyphenols (plant chemicals) it contains, an alarming number of us find it difficult to stop at one small glass. After all, it seems such a tiny amount.

We all know that large amounts of alcohol can lead to alcoholism and liver disease. It can also increase your risk of cardiovascular disease, and contribute to obesity and diabetes.

The recommended maximum intake of alcohol is two units per day for women, and three per day for men, and you should also have two or three alcohol-free days each week. Binge drinking is especially harmful, so don't be tempted to save up your units for the weekend or a big party!

For some really easy bites, try:

- Cocktail oatcakes or water biscuits topped with low-fat soft cheese and a little smoked salmon.
- Pickled onions, gherkins and pineapple cubes speared on cocktail sticks – leave out the cheese!

What's a unit?

- Half a pint of average-strength beer, lager or cider (3–4% alcohol by volume – ABV)
- A small glass of wine (9% ABV)
- A standard pub measure (25ml) of spirits (40% ABV)
- A standard pub measure (50ml) of fortified wine, e.g. sherry, port (20% ABV)
- Cans of beer and lager often contain about three-quarters of a pint, rather than half, and so will contain 1.5 units – and more if it's a high-strength brew.

It's also easy to tot up two units in one drink. All of the following equal approximately two units:

- A pint or a large can (500ml) of average strength beer, lager or cider (3–4% ABV)
- Half a pint or half a large can of high-strength beer or lager (8–9% ABV)
- A large measure (50ml) of spirits
- A large glass (175ml) of wine that is 11–12% ABV
- A 330ml bottle of lager or alco-pop (5.5% ABV)

If you're going to drink . . .

- **Go slowly – no more than one unit per hour.**
  The ethanol in alcoholic drinks is a toxin, so as soon as it's absorbed, it's sent straight to the liver to be detoxified. If alcohol arrives faster than the liver can handle it, it returns to the bloodstream.

- **Don't drink on an empty stomach.**
  Food slows the absorption of alcohol. Not only will this slow down the rate at which the alcohol hits your system, it will also smooth out the rise in blood sugar caused by drinking alcohol.

- **Alternate alcoholic drinks with non-alcoholic ones.**
  Not only will this slow down your drinking, limiting the amount of alcohol you consume, it will help to rehydrate you. Alcohol is a potent diuretic, and will quickly lead to dehydrating. And dehydration makes you feel rough – headaches, dizziness . . . Does any of that sound familiar?

- **Stick to one kind of drink.**
  All alcohol counts towards your 'units' total, but mixing your drinks can increase your chances of having a horrendous hangover the next morning. The saying 'don't mix the grape and the grain' is based on sound science. So, don't mix spirits and wine in an evening.

And those units add up surprisingly quickly. Many people wrongly believe that a glass of wine equals a unit, simple as that. But that's a small glass of wine, not the large glasses that many pubs and restaurants now serve as standard, which can double or even triple your tally.

Also remember that measures served at home tend to be more generous than pub measures, and cocktails can contain four or five units in a single drink!

ANOTHER REASON TO BEWARE THE BOOZE

Many people are surprised at how many calories there are in their drinks. A gram of alcohol contains seven calories. That's more than a gram of protein or carbohydrate – only fat has more!

So, it's surprisingly easy to pile on the pounds by knocking back a few drinks! Here are the calorie counts of a few popular tipples:

Beers, lager and cider (per half pint)

Bitter	90 calories
Mild	71 calories
Pale ale	91 calories
Brown ale	80 calories
Stout	105 calories
Lager – ordinary strength	85 calories
Dry cider	95 calories
Sweet cider	110 calories

Wine (125ml glass)

Red wine	85 calories
Rosé wine	89 calories
White wine (sweet)	118 calories
White wine (medium)	94 calories
White wine (dry)	83 calories
Sparkling white wine	95 calories

Fortified wine (50ml measure)

Port	79 calories
Sherry (dry)	58 calories

Spirits (25ml pub measure)

Gin, vodka, whisky, brandy, rum etc.	52 calories

Liqueurs, being so high in sugar, are the most calorific. And don't forget the mixers – juice, cola, lemonade and the like can really make the sugar and calorie count add up.

ACTION
PUT ON YOUR DANCING SHOES

Dancing is fantastic exercise for all ages. It's fun, you meet people, the clothes are great, your tensions float away as you glide, shimmy or bop your way across the dance floor . . . and it doesn't even feel like exercise.

Dancing has been given a whole new lease of life by the popular TV dancing programmes of the past couple of years.

Don't worry if your last memories of dancing are pirouetting in a pink tutu at the age of six. Dancing classes have come a long way, but if you missed ballet or tap dancing as a child many dancing schools have adult ballet and tap classes for beginners. Or you might prefer the New York City Ballet workout – it's very trendy, and many areas now offer classes.

The variety of dance classes for adults is extensive – from the sedate to the exhilarating – so you're sure to be able to find something to get you moving, from sensuous belly dancing and sizzling salsa, to intricate line dancing, and not forgetting modern dance and ballroom.

Check out your library and local newspapers for details of classes. If you're not sure that a style of dancing is for you, ask if you can watch a class before joining. Don't worry if you haven't got a partner, you'll still be welcome at most classes.

But if you can't find time to get to a class there's no excuse not to dance. There are scores of videos out there, from 'teach yourself' ballroom or Latin American dancing, to dance-based workouts, based on a variety of music styles, from Jazzercise to hip-hop. Just choose the kind of dancing you'd like to try, put on the video and away you go. You never know, you might get so enthusiastic that you decide to find time to join a class.

MENU PLANNER
DECEMBER IDEAS

 **DECEMBER BEST BUYS**

Make the most of:

Pears

Cranberries

Celery

Cauliflower

Brussels sprouts

Celeriac

Red cabbage

Swede

Pumpkin

Menu 1

 **Breakfast**   Christmas fruit cocktail platter

 Lunch   Christmas turkey lunch

Christmas Trifles

 Dinner   Prawn and cress salad with herb croutons

Menu 2

☀ **Breakfast**   Devilled mushrooms on wholemeal toast

☀ **Lunch**   Christmas calzone

☾ **Dinner**   Spiced baked fish with cucumber and pepper salsa

Roast spiced plums with orange yogurt cream and ratafias

Menu 1
☼ Christmas fruit cocktail platter

Prepare these fruits ahead and lay out on a platter ready for Christmas morning. There is a lot of eating in the day ahead so start with something light and cleansing.

1   Using a sharp knife, slice off the top and bases of each grapefruit, then place the fruits on a board and cut off the peel and pith. Take up each fruit in turn, hold over a bowl and slice down between the dividing membranes, loosening the segments so they fall into the bowl along with any juice.

2   Halve the pomegranate. Break open each half into segments then pick off the juicy seeds into another bowl, discarding the creamy-coloured membranes. Blitz half the seeds in a blender until juicy. Strain over the grapefruit. Reserve the other half of seeds.

3   Quarter, core and slice the apples. Peel, deseed and cut the melon into chunks or scoop into balls. Peel and quarter the kiwis. Mix all the fruits together and chill until ready to serve.

4   Stir the cinnamon with the lemon zest. Spoon the fruits out onto a large platter and sprinkle over the lemon-cinnamon mixture, then serve.

Health fact: This breakfast is a powerhouse of antioxidants – remember that it's best to eat a variety of colours of fruit, and there's certainly a selection here! Natural fruit sugars provide energy, while the fibre in the fruit helps you feel full for longer.

2 pink grapefruits

1 pomegranate

2 red-skinned apples

1 small ripe melon of your choice

2 kiwi fruits

1tsp cinnamon

Grated zest of 1 lemon

Serves 6

☼ Christmas turkey lunch

1 turkey crown (i.e. breast on the bone) roast joint (2–2.4kg), thawed if frozen

Sprigs of fresh thyme, sage or rosemary

5–6tbsp olive oil

1tsp ground paprika

1tbsp flour

2–3 tbsp white or red wine

300ml stock (made with a cube)

A little sea salt and freshly ground black pepper

For the crumb dressing:

100g fresh wholemeal bread crumbs

Grated zest of 1 lemon and a little juice for the gravy

2 fat cloves of garlic, finely chopped

2tsp leaves fresh thyme or 1tbsp chopped fresh sage

25g each chopped roasted hazelnuts, sunflower and pumpkin seeds

For the roasted potatoes and sprouts:

500g sweet potatoes

1kg potatoes (Maris Piper, Desiree or King Edwards)

500g Brussels sprouts

Small knob of butter

2tbsp chopped fresh parsley

Serves 6

Turkey is a very healthy low-fat meat, so keep the trimmings healthy too. Serve roast sweet potatoes as well as potatoes, sprouts cooked just at the last minute so they remain sweet and delicious, and American-style crunchy bread dressing rather than heavy stuffing. Total cooking time will be around 2 hours for this meal, although the crumb dressing and vegetables can be prepared ahead.

1 Make the dressing first – heat the oven to 190°C/Gas 5. Mix together the breadcrumbs, 2tbsp oil, lemon zest, garlic, thyme or chopped sage leaves, nuts, seeds and pepper to taste (no salt needed). Tip into a shallow ovenproof tin and cook for about 25 minutes, stirring once or twice, until browned and crunchy. Remove and reserve.

2 To cook the turkey – work your fingers between the skin and flesh on the top of the joint and push in 2–3 sprigs fresh thyme, sage or rosemary on each side. Mix 1tbsp oil with the paprika to a paste and spread over the turkey breasts. Season with pepper only and cover loosely with a sheet of foil. Cook at 190°C/Gas 5 for about 1? hours or until the meat feels firm when pressed and a skewer inserted in the thickest part gives off colourless juices. Remove the foil after 1 hour to allow the skin to crisp. When the turkey is cooked, set it to rest in a warm place, covered again with the foil – it will stay warm for a good half-hour and is easier to carve. Reserve the pan juices for the gravy.

3 For the potatoes and sweet potatoes – peel and cut both into big bite-sized chunks. Blanch in a pan of boiling water for 5 minutes then drain well and return to the pan. Stir in 2–3tbsp more oil to coat all sides. Shake out onto a roasting pan and season lightly. Roast on a shelf above the turkey for about 30 minutes, turning once until crispy and browned.

4 To make the gravy – return the turkey-roasting pan with the cooking juices to the hob and stir in the wine for 30 seconds, then mix in the flour. Cook for 1 minute then gradually work in the stock, stirring until thickened. Season, add a squeeze of lemon juice and strain into a jug or gravy boat.

5 For the sprouts – cook just before serving so they remain sweet tasting, Boil in water for just 5 minutes then drain and run immediately under cold water. Tip back into the pan with a knob of butter and chopped parsley, plus seasoning to taste. Serve as soon as possible.

Health fact: Turkey is a great low-fat protein food – it has 30 per cent fewer calories and 50 per cent less fat than beef, and sweet potatoes are packed full of betacarotene and other antioxidants.

Brussels sprouts are one of the best vegetable sources of vitamin C. They also contain phytochemicals that may protect against bowel cancer.

Christmas trifles

75g pack dried cranberries

1 can (425g) apricots or peaches in natural juice

300ml cranberry juice

2tbsp port, optional

2 sheets leaf gelatine or 1½ tsp gelatine crystals

1tbsp custard powder

1tbsp sugar or 1½ tsp fructose

300ml skimmed milk

200g tub lemon, vanilla or toffee non-fat yogurt

8 ginger nuts or 6 digestive biscuits

Serves 6

Make lighter versions of this great family favourite dessert and serve spooned into wine or Champagne glasses.

1 Soak the dried cranberries in hot water for 10 minutes, then drain and set aside. Drain the juice from the fruits into a saucepan. Roughly chop the drained fruit and mix with two-thirds of the cranberries and chill. Reserve the remaining cranberries to decorate at the end. Add the cranberry juice and port to the fruit juice in the saucepan then boil until reduced down to about 300ml.

2 Meanwhile, halve the gelatine sheets and submerge in a bowl of cold water until floppy. Drain and squeeze out excess water.

3 When the juice is reduced, remove from the heat and stir in the gelatine – either soaked leaves or sprinkle over the crystals, stirring until dissolved. Pour the liquid into a shallow container, cool and chill until set.

4 Make the custard. Blend the powder and sugar in a cup with about 2tbsp of the milk. Heat the rest until on the point of boiling. Pour some of this hot milk into the cup and stir to mix, then return both to the pan and heat again, stirring, until thickened.

5 Remove and cool, stirring once or twice to stop a skin forming. Chill until required.

6 When ready to assemble, demould the jelly onto a clean board and chop into small pieces.

7 Roughly crush the biscuits into large crumbs, either by beating them in a sealed bag with a rolling pin, or pulsing in a food processor. Mix two-thirds of the crumbs with the soaked cranberries and chopped fruit, and divide between 6 wine or sundae glasses. Spoon over two-thirds of the jelly.

8 Stir together the cold custard and yogurt, which should thicken slightly. Spoon these over the jelly. Divide the remaining jelly on top and scatter with the last of the biscuit crumbs and the saved cranberries. Serve lightly chilled.

Health fact: Most Christmas desserts are loaded with fat and sugar, but this one is much more virtuous! By using the juice from the canned fruits, you retain much of their nutrients. And the skimmed milk provides protein and calcium, without piling on the fat.

Prawn and cress salad with herb croutons

This is ideal for a light supper on Christmas night. Instead of high-fat shop-bought croutons, make your own quickly using wholemeal bread and olive oil. Instead of prawns you could substitute smoked salmon.

1. Make the croutons first. Preheat the oven to 180°C/Gas 4. Cut the crustless bread into small pieces, roughly 1cm square. Pop into a large food bag. Drizzle in the oil and add the herbs plus some seasoning to taste, if liked. Seal the bag and shake well to coat the bread cubes, then tip out onto a shallow roasting tin and bake for 12–15 minutes until crisp. Remove and cool.
2. Pat the prawns dry with paper towel. Shake over some dashes of pepper sauce, if liked.
3. When ready to serve, beat together the vinaigrette and crème fraîche then toss with the salad leaves. Divide between 6 shallow bowls or plates and spoon over the prawns. Serve with lemon wedges andscatter over the croutons.

Health fact: Watercress is rich in iron and vitamins. Dark-green salad leaves such as rocket and baby leaf spinach are much higher in vitamins than paler lettuce varieties.

400g frozen large prawns, thawed

Tabasco, to shake, optional

2x200g bags mixed watercress and spinach leaves or 1 pack each baby leaf spinach and rocket

5tbsp vinaigrette

2tbsp reduced-fat crème fraîche

1 lemon, cut in 6 wedges

Sea salt and freshly ground black pepper

For the croutons:

3 slices wholemeal bread, crusts cut off

2tbsp olive oil

1tsp dried oregano or mixed herbs

Serves 6

Menu 2
☼ Devilled mushrooms on wholemeal toast

1tsp olive oil

350g button mushrooms

4 tomatoes, skinned and chopped

2 spring onions, chopped

1tbsp tomato purée

2tbsp water

1tbsp Worcestershire sauce

4 slices wholemeal bread, toasted

1tbsp parsley, chopped

Serves 4

1 Wipe a nonstick pan with water, leaving a few drops behind, instead of oil. Wipe and quarter the mushrooms and sauté very gently with the tomatoes and the spring onions in the pan until they are tender.

2 Add the tomato purée, water and Worcestershire sauce to the pan and stir. Cook for a further minute.

3 Meanwhile, toast the bread, and spoon over the devilled mushrooms. Sprinkle over the parsley and serve immediately.

Health fact: Mushrooms contain useful amounts of B-vitamins, as well as phosphorus and potassium. Wholemeal bread supplies energy in a slow-release form to sustain you through the morning.

☼ Christmas calzone

Calzone is an Italian folded pizza, and a family-size one makes a great special Christmas dish filled with ratatouille and diced mozzarella. Choose a bread mix with herbs or grains.

1   First make the filling so it can cool ahead. Sauté the aubergine, pepper, onion and garlic in 3tbsp of the oil until just softened, about 10 minutes. Stir in the tomatoes, capers (if using) and sprouts and season lightly. Simmer for about 10 more minutes or until the liquid has reduced right down. Remove and cool.

2   Make up the bread mix according to pack instructions, allowing to rise just once in the mixing bowl. When doubled in volume, punch down and knead on a lightly floured board until smooth. Roll out to a rough circle, approximately 35cm. It doesn't have to be too neat.

3   Lift the dough over the rolling pin onto a large nonstick baking sheet or one lined with baking parchment. Brush around the edges with cold water.

4   Pile the vegetable filling onto one side and sprinkle over the cheese, pressing it into the vegetables.

5   Lift over the unfilled half and press down around the edges, folding over and pinching to seal. It doesn't matter if it looks quite rustic. Slash the top 3 or 4 times with a sharp knife and brush with the last spoon of oil. Scatter over the thyme sprigs or chopped rosemary.

6   Preheat the oven while the calzone rests for 15 minutes to 200°C/Gas 6, then bake for about 20 minutes until risen and golden brown. Slide the calzone onto a wire tray to cool for 15 minutes then place onto a platter or board to serve.

Health fact: All those colourful vegetables – peppers, aubergines and tomatoes – provide a variety of antioxidants, which help prevent damage to the body's cells by harmful free radicals. The cheese provides protein, plus calcium for healthy bones.

1x500g pack bread mix

4–5 sprigs fresh thyme or 1tbsp chopped fresh rosemary

For the filling:

1 small aubergine, chopped small

1 yellow pepper, cored and diced

1 onion, chopped

3 fat cloves of garlic, crushed

4tbsp olive oil

1 can (400g) chopped tomatoes with herbs

2tbsp capers, optional

100g bean or lentil sprouts

150g mozzarella or goats' cheese, diced or crumbled

Sea salt and freshly ground black pepper

Serves 4

☾ Spiced baked fish with cucumber and pepper salsa

800g–1kg fillet of salmon or 2 smaller fillets of cod or haddock

2 fat cloves of garlic, crushed

2cm cube fresh root ginger, grated

3tbsp olive or sunflower oil

1tsp curry powder

Sea salt and freshly ground black pepper

For the salsa:

½ a cucumber

2 spring onions, finely chopped

1 small green pepper, cored and finely chopped

2 ripe tomatoes, finely chopped, optional

1tsp ground cumin

1tbsp white wine vinegar

4tbsp chopped fresh herbs, mixture of parsley, mint and coriander

3tbsp natural yogurt, optional

Serves 6

This recipe is not only easy to prepare, but it has a tasty spicy twist. Serve with a crisp chopped salad relish and a bowl of brown basmati rice, crusty brown bread or creamy mashed potatoes and celeriac.

1   First, make the salsa ahead. Slit the cucumber and scoop out the seeds with a teaspoon, then chop the flesh into small dice. Put into a bowl with the onions, pepper, tomatoes, cumin, vinegar and ½tsp salt plus pepper to taste. Stir and set aside for an hour until ready to cook the fish.

2   Check the fish for bones with your fingers and pull out any stray ones. Place in a large roasting tin. Mix together the garlic, ginger, oil and curry powder to a paste and spread over the fish with the back of a spoon. Leave for 30 minutes to marinate.

3   When ready to cook, heat the oven to 190°C/Gas 5 and bake the fish for about 18–20 minutes or until the top feels firm when pressed. Remove and cool for 10 minutes before serving. For a creamier salsa, drain away most of the juices that form and mix in the yogurt.

Health fact: This is a heart-healthy dish – salmon is rich in omega-3 fatty acids, which help make the blood less 'sticky', while if you use cod or haddock these are very low in fat. Red and green peppers are packed with antioxidants, which help prevent heart disease.

Roast spiced plums with orange yogurt and ratafias

Cook these plums ahead and serve at room temperature.

1 Preheat the oven to 200°C/Gas 6. Halve the plums and remove the stones. Lay cut side up in a shallow ovenproof dish. Mix together the icing sugar and spice and sprinkle over the plums. Bake for 15–20 minutes until the plum tops brown and bubble. Remove and cool.

2 Mix together the yogurt, honey (to taste), orange zest and juice. Serve with the plums and ratafias.

Health fact: Red and purple plums are a good source of the antioxidant plant chemicals called anthocyanins, which help protect the body's cells from damage.

6 large ripe red plums

1tbsp icing sugar

1tsp mixed spice

1 tub (200g) 0%-fat Greek yogurt

1–2tbsp runny honey

Grated zest and juice of 1 orange

24–30 baby-size ratafias (about 50g)

Serves 6

QUICK RECIPES

MAIN COURSES

Pork and cabbage stir-fry

2tbsp sunflower oil

400g pork tenderloin or boneless leg, trimmed and thinly sliced

2 green peppers, deseeded and thinly sliced

1 medium fennel head, trimmed and chopped

2–3tsp fennel seeds (or to taste)

2tsp prepared crushed garlic

400g chestnut or button mushrooms, wiped, trimmed and thinly sliced

100ml ready-made vegetable stock or water

1½ tbsp organic wheat-free tamari soy sauce

200g savoy cabbage, cored and finely shredded (about 155g prepared weight)

250g cooked and cooled brown basmati rice

Salt and freshly ground black pepper (optional)

4tbsp chopped fresh parsley

Tabasco sauce, to serve (optional)

Serves 4

1 Heat a wok or large frying pan, ideally nonstick, over a high heat until a splash of water 'dances' on the surface. Add 1 tablespoon of the oil and heat until it shimmers, swirling it around the side.

2 Add the pork to the wok and stir for 2–3 minutes until it is cooked through and the juices run clear when you cut a piece. Use a slotted spoon to remove the pork and set aside.

3 Add the remaining oil to the wok and heat. Add the green peppers, fennel, fennel seeds and garlic and stir-fry for 2 minutes. Stir in the mushrooms and continue stirring for about 3 minutes until they soften and start to give off their liquid.

4 Stir in the stock or water and soy sauce and bring to the boil. Add the cabbage, continue stir-frying until it wilts and three-quarters of the liquid has evaporated.

5 Add the rice to the wok and stir around until heated through and the remaining liquid has evaporated. Taste and adjust the seasoning if necessary. Stir in the parsley and serve at once with a sprinkling of Tabasco sauce if you like.

Chicken, mushroom and sweet corn stir-fry

1tbsp cornflour

1tbsp organic wheat-free tamari soy sauce

125ml ready-made vegetable stock or water

1½ tbsp sunflower or corn oil

4 boneless, skinless chicken thighs, about 85g each, thinly sliced

1 medium onion, peeled and chopped

2 celery sticks, trimmed and thinly sliced

1tsp prepared chopped garlic

1tsp prepared chopped ginger

200g button mushrooms, wiped, trimmed and thinly sliced

1 can (195g) sweet-corn kernels in water, drained

300g ready-to-cook Chinese egg noodles

Chopped fresh coriander, to garnish

Serves 4

1 Put the cornflour in a small bowl and stir in the tamari soy sauce. Slowly stir in the stock or water until no lumps remain, then set aside.

2 Heat a wok or large frying pan, ideally nonstick, over a high heat until a splash of water 'dances' on the surface. Add 1 tablespoon of the oil and heat until it shimmers, swirling it around the side. Add the chicken and stir-fry for 2–3 minutes until it is cooked through and the juices run clear when you cut a piece, Use a slotted spoon to remove the chicken and set aside.

3 Add the remaining half-tablespoon of oil and heat. Add the onion, celery, garlic and ginger and stir-fry for 1 minute. Add the mushrooms and continue stir-frying for about 2 minutes longer until the mushrooms are soft and beginning to give off liquid. Stir in the corn kernels and return the chicken to the wok.

4 Pour the cornflour mixture into the wok and stir until it thickens. Add the egg noodles to the wok, then use 2 wooden forks to mix all the ingredients together. Continue stir-frying until the noodles are hot. Sprinkle with coriander and serve at once.

Lamb and black bean stir-fry

1 Heat a wok or large frying pan, ideally nonstick, over a high heat until a splash of water 'dances' on the surface. Add 1 tablespoon of the oil and heat until it shimmers, swirling it around the side. Add the lamb and stir-fry for 2–3 minutes until the pieces brown, but are still pink on the inside. Use a slotted spoon to remove the lamb and set aside.

2 Add the remaining half-tablespoon of oil and heat. Add the red pepper and stir-fry for 1 minute. Add the leeks, snow peas or green beans and continue stir-frying for about 2 minutes until the red peppers are soft.

3 Stir the black bean sauce and vinegar if liked and bring to the boil. Stir in the lamb, bean sprouts and noodles and use 2 forks to mix all the ingredients together. Sprinkle with the mint leaves and sesame seeds and serve at once.

1½ tbsp sunflower oil

350g boneless leg of lamb or fillet, trimmed and thinly sliced

2 large red peppers, deseeded and sliced

1tsp prepared crushed garlic

2 medium leeks, trimmed, thinly sliced, rinsed and shaken dry

155g snow peas, trimmed and halved, or 155g green beans, trimmed and chopped

100g sachet black bean stir-fry sauce

½ tbsp rice wine vinegar or dry sherry (optional)

85g fresh bean sprouts, rinsed and dried

300g ready-to-cook Chinese egg noodles

2tbsp torn fresh mint leaves

1tbsp sesame seeds, toasted

Serves 4

Glazed lamb chops with crushed peas

1 Preheat a grill until hot. Brush oil over both sides of the chops. Lay on a grill pan and season lightly. Turn the heat to medium and grill for 5 minutes.

2 Mix together the jelly and mint. Turn the chops and spread with the jelly. Return to the heat for another 5 minutes then remove and stand for 5 minutes.

3 Meanwhile, boil the peas according to pack instructions. Drain, return to the pan with the fat spread and crush with a potato masher or fork.

4 To serve, squeeze the chops with the lime quarters and serve alongside the peas. Boiled new potatoes are perfect with this.

8 loin lamb chops or 4x100g chump chops, trimmed of fat

1tbsp olive or sunflower oil

2tbsp redcurrant jelly

2tbsp chopped fresh mint (or 1tsp dried)

250g frozen peas

1tsp low-fat spread

1 lime, cut in quarters

Sea salt and freshly ground black pepper

Serves 4

Pork and courgette stroganoff

1 Fry the onion and garlic in the oil until softened and lightly browned, about 10 minutes. Push the onions aside in the pan and stir in the pork until lightly browned, about 3 minutes.

2 Add the courgettes and cook for 2 minutes, then stir in the stock and tomato purée or mustard. Season lightly, bring to a simmer and cook for 3–5 minutes more until reduced down slightly.

3 Mix in the soured cream or crème fraîche and bubble for a minute or so. Serve hot with green tagliatelle or boiled potatoes.

1 large red onion, halved and sliced

2–3 fat cloves of garlic, crushed or chopped

3tbsp olive or sunflower oil

400g lean pork, sliced in thin strips

1 medium courgette, cut in medium thick sticks

300ml stock (made from a cube)

1tbsp tomato purée or 2tbsp grain mustard

1x142ml pot soured cream or 150g reduced-fat crème fraîche

Sea salt and freshly ground black pepper

Serves 4

LIGHT SNACKS AND MEAL SALADS

Egg salad pitta pockets

1 free-range egg, hard boiled

2tsp light mayonnaise

A good pinch of curry powder

1 wholemeal pitta bread, plain or flavoured

2–3 little gem lettuce leaves

Sea salt and freshly ground black pepper

Serves 1

1. Peel and chop the egg in a small bowl. Mix with the mayonnaise and curry powder. Season lightly if liked.
2. Halve the pitta and open up with your fingers, trying not to split it.
3. Stuff the lettuce leaves inside, breaking to fit. Spoon in the egg salad and press together. Wrap in clingfilm until required.

Smoked chicken and mandarin salad

1 can (300g) mandarin segments in juice

1tsp dried ginger

1tsp toasted sesame oil

1tsp rice wine vinegar or dry sherry

200g mixed salad greens, such as escarole, endive, radicchio and tatsoi, or baby spinach leaves, rinsed and patted dry

175g boneless, skinless smoked chicken, or cooked ham, cut into bite-sized pieces

6 spring onions, trimmed and shredded

1 large carrot, peeled and grated

1 red pepper, deseeded and very finely sliced with a vegetable peeler

Leaves from 4 sprigs of fresh flat-leaf parsley or coriander, coarsely torn

2tbsp toasted sesame seeds

Serves 4

1. Strain the mandarin segments, reserving the juice.
2. Put the dried ginger in a large salad bowl, then stir in the sesame oil, rice wine vinegar and 3 tablespoons of the reserved mandarin juice. (The remaining juice can be drunk or added to smoothies or fruit salads.)
3. Add the salad greens to the bowl and toss in the dressing until all the leaves are lightly coated. Add the smoked chicken, spring onions, carrot, red pepper and herb leaves and toss again.
4. Divide between 4 bowls and sprinkle with sesame seeds.

Italian tuna and bean salad

1 can (200g) tuna in spring water, drained and flaked into chunky pieces

1 can (400g) cannellini or butter beans, drained, rinsed and patted dry

4 peeled red peppers in olive oil, drained and sliced

2 spring onions, trimmed and finely sliced

2tbsp fruity olive oil

1tbsp balsamic vinegar

1 cos lettuce, cored and shredded

Coarse sea salt and freshly ground black pepper

Chopped fresh parsley or dill, to garnish

Wholemeal rolls, to serve

Serves 4

1. Put the tuna, beans, red peppers and spring onions in a bowl. Add the olive oil, vinegar and salt and pepper to taste and gently toss together, taking care not to break up the tuna too much. Cover and chill for several hours or serve at once.
2. Remove the salad from the fridge 10–15 minutes before serving to bring to room temperature. To serve, divide the lettuce between 4 plates and top with the salad mixture. Sprinkle with fresh parsley or dill.

SALADS, STARTERS AND ACCOMPANIMENTS

Rainbow coleslaw

1 Cut the cabbage in half through its length and remove the outside leaves and central core.
2 Slice the cabbage, apple and celery into a salad bowl. Grate the carrots and onion and add to the bowl. Add the chopped walnuts, with the oil and vinegar, to the bowl.
3 Season with ground black pepper. Toss well together and serve.

¼ of a red cabbage
1 apple, quartered and cored
4 celery sticks, trimmed
4 medium carrots, peeled
½ a small red onion, peeled and quartered
50g walnut halves, roughly chopped
50g sultanas
4tbsp extra virgin olive oil
1tbsp cider vinegar
Freshly ground black pepper
Serves 4 as an accompaniment

Simple Caesar salad

1 Toast the bread until golden then rub on both sides with the garlic. Cut into 1cm cubes and set aside.
2 Separate the lettuce leaves and discard the central core. Wash the lettuce well under cold running water.
3 Divide the lettuce leaves between 4 plates. Peel the eggs and cut into quarters. Place on top of the leaves and scatter with the toasted garlic bread. Sprinkle with the Parmesan.
4 Put all the mayonnaise and parsley in a small bowl with 1tbsp cold water and mix well. Spoon over the salad to serve.

1 slice wholegrain bread
1 garlic clove, peeled and halved
1 cos lettuce, any damaged leaves removed
3 medium eggs, hard boiled
15g Parmesan cheese, finely grated
For the dressing:
20g low-fat mayonnaise
2tsp freshly chopped parsley
Serves 4 as a starter

Fresh tomato salsa

1 Place the onion, garlic and chilli into a blender and blend for a few seconds until roughly chopped.
2 Remove the lid and add the tomatoes, coriander and a little freshly ground black pepper. Replace the lid and blend on maximum for just a few seconds until the tomatoes and coriander are roughly chopped.
3 Remove the blade and spoon the mixture into a serving dish. Cover and chill for about an hour before serving.
4 Serve with lots of fresh vegetable sticks or wholemeal pitta bread for dipping. This recipe will keep well for up to 2 days. Cover and keep in the fridge.

½ a small red onion, quartered
1 garlic clove, peeled and halved
1 red chilli, halved, deseeded and roughly chopped
250g ripe tomatoes, quartered
1 small bunch fresh coriander (about 10g)
Freshly ground black pepper
Vegetable sticks or toasted wholemeal pitta bread, to serve
Serves 4–6

Tabbouleh

115g bulgur wheat

Large bunch of fresh mint (about 50g)

Large bunch of fresh flat-leaf parsley (about 50g)

3 large ripe tomatoes, chopped

4 spring onions, trimmed and sliced

2tbsp extra virgin olive oil

Freshly squeezed juice and finely grated zest of 1 lemon

Freshly ground black pepper

Serves 4–6 as an accompaniment

1 Cook the bulgur wheat in boiling water according to the pack instructions. Drain and rinse in a sieve under cold running water; set aside.

2 Place the mint and parsley in a colander and wash under cold running water. Dry the herbs and roughly chop.

3 Put the herbs, tomatoes, onion, olive oil and lemon juice and zest in a large bowl. Add the bulgur wheat and toss well together. Season with black pepper and serve.

Grilled red pepper houmous

1 large red pepper, halved and deseeded

1 can (410g) 'no-salt' chickpeas, drained and rinsed

4 spring onions, trimmed and roughly chopped

1 garlic clove, peeled and quartered

3tbsp tahini (sesame seed paste), drained of oil before measuring

½ tsp organic vegetable bouillon (stock) powder

2tbsp freshly squeezed lemon juice

4tbsp cold water

Freshly ground black pepper

Fresh assorted vegetable sticks, to serve

Serves 6–8 as a dip

1 Place the pepper cut-side down on a grill pan. Cook under a preheated hot grill for about 10 minutes until the skin blackens and blisters. Remove from the grill using a fork, place in a bowl and cover with clingfilm. Leave to cool for 20 minutes before handling.

2 Place the pepper on a board and remove the skin. Put the pepper in a food processor with all the remaining ingredients and season with ground black pepper. Blend until smooth.

3 Remove the blade and spoon the houmous into a serving dish.

Serve with plenty of assorted vegetable sticks for dipping.

SNACKS AND NIBBLES
Soy snack mix

25g pumpkin seeds

25g pine nuts

25g sunflower seeds

2tbsp sesame seeds

1tsp organic wheat-free tamari soy sauce

Serves 4

1 Preheat the oven to 200°C/Gas 6. Place all the seeds in a bowl and stir in the soy sauce until thoroughly mixed. Sprinkle onto a tray lined with foil and spread evenly.

2 Bake for just 4 minutes until all the seeds are very lightly browned. Remove from the oven and allow to cool and become crisp. Tip into a bowl and serve. Eat within 24 hours.

Pesto pitta bread crisps

1 Preheat the oven to 200°C/Gas 6. Place the pitta bread on a baking tray and put in the oven to warm for a minute. Remove and cool for a couple of minutes before carefully slicing in half horizontally – through the side – and opening up.

2 Cut each of the halves into five triangles using scissors. Return to the tray rough-side down and brush with the pesto sauce. Bake for 5–6 minutes until pale golden brown. Leave on the tray to cool and crisp up before serving. (These are best eaten on the day they are prepared.)

> **Health fact:** Wholemeal pitta bread contains more fibre than white, so will take longer to digest and will sustain your energy levels better – as well as promoting a healthier digestion. These crunchy snacks are perfect for dipping and contain far less fat and salt than traditional snacks such as potato crisps or tortilla chips.

2 wholemeal pitta bread
2tsp green pesto sauce
Serves 4

SWEET TREATS

An occasional sweet treat won't hurt you – and these are much healthier, and lower in fat and sugar, than most of those you'll buy in the shops.

Fruited pecan and banana tea loaf

1 Put the tea bag in a bowl and pour over the water. Infuse for 2–3 minutes, then remove the tea bag and stir in the raisins, sultanas, prunes and mixed spice. Stand for 15 minutes, stirring occasionally.

2 Preheat the oven to 160°C/Gas 3. Lightly oil a 900g nonstick loaf tin and line the base with baking parchment. Break the eggs into a bowl and add the oil, sugar, flour, baking powder and banana. Beat with a wooden spoon until smooth.

3 Stir the pecan nuts into the flour-and-egg mixture, then add to the soaked dried-fruit mixture and stir well together. Spoon into the prepared tin and smooth the surface.

4 Bake for 1–1¼ hours until risen and pale golden brown. Cover loosely with a piece of foil for the last 30 minutes of cooking time to prevent over-browning. Check the cake is ready by inserting a skewer into the centre – it should come out clean.

1 Earl Grey tea bag
100ml just-boiled water
200g raisins
200g sultanas
200g 'ready-to-eat' prunes, chopped
1tsp ground mixed spice
2 medium free-range eggs
3tbsp sunflower oil
50g unrefined light brown muscovado sugar
175g wholemeal plain flour
1tsp baking powder
1 small banana (100g peeled weight), mashed well with a fork
50g shelled pecan nuts, roughly chopped
Makes 12 slices

250g fresh dates, stoned and halved

300ml pressed apple juice

3tbsp sunflower oil, plus a little extra for greasing

50g plain wholemeal flour

200g jumbo or organic porridge oats

50g desiccated coconut

Makes 16 pieces

Sticky oat and date slice

1 Preheat the oven to 200°C/Gas 6. Lightly oil a 20cm loose-based square cake tin. Put the dates and half of the apple juice in a small pan. Bring to the boil, then reduce the heat and cook gently for 8–10 minutes until the dates are well softened, stirring occasionally. Set aside.

2 Mix the remaining apple juice with the sunflower oil. Stir the flour, porridge oats and coconut together in a large bowl. Pour over the apple juice and sunflower-oil mixture and stir well. Stand for 5 minutes, stirring occasionally until all the apple juice has been soaked up.

3 Spoon half the oat mixture into the prepared tin and press down well with the back of a dessertspoon. Stir the softened dates vigorously with a wooden spoon until they turn into a thick paste – making it as smooth as possible.

4 Drop spoonfuls of the paste onto the oat mixture, then spread gently with the back of a spoon, leaving a 1cm border around the edge. (Try to keep the spoon in contact with the dates to help prevent the oats from lifting.)

5 Sprinkle with the remaining oat mixture and pat down well. Bake for 20–25 minutes until golden brown. Remove from the oven and leave to cool in the tin for 15 minutes. Carefully remove from the tin and leave to cool. Cut into squares to serve.

75g walnut halves

2 medium carrots, peeled (about 140g)

6 fresh dates, stoned and halved

3 medium free-range eggs

40g light muscovado sugar

5tbsp sunflower oil, plus extra for greasing

175g wholemeal flour

1tsp baking powder

1tsp ground mixed spice

Makes 10 slices

Date, carrot and walnut cake

1 Preheat the oven to 180°C/Gas 4. Lightly oil and line the base of a 900g nonstick loaf tin (base measuring 19x9cm) with baking parchment.

2 Roughly chop 25g of the nuts and put to one side. Grate the carrots and put to one side.

3 Put the walnuts, dates, eggs, sugar, oil, flour, baking powder and spice in a bowl and blend together well.

4 Add the carrots to the mixture and combine well. Spoon the mixture into the prepared tin. Sprinkle with the reserved nuts and bake for 1 hour until golden brown and firm to the touch. Cover loosely with foil for the last 20 minutes cooking time to prevent over-browning.

5 Leave to stand for a few minutes in the tin, then turn out onto a wire rack to cool. Serve just warm or cold in slices.

Dark chocolate fondue with fresh fruit dippers

100g dark chocolate, at least 70% cocoa solids

6tbsp fresh orange juice or water

Selection of whole ripe strawberries or pineapple chunks or a just-ripe kiwi fruit

Serves 4

1. Break up the chocolate into a large ramekin or small bowl. Add the orange juice or water. Melt in the microwave on a medium power setting for 2–3 minutes and stir until smooth. Set aside for 5 minutes while you prepare the fruits.
2. Wash the strawberries, if necessary, but pat dry immediately. Hull if liked. Peel the kiwi and cut into quarters. Pat dry the pineapple with paper towel.
3. Serve the chocolate fondue bowl on a plate surrounded by the fruits. Use a fork to dip the fruits into the chocolate.

Health fact: Dark chocolate contains plant chemicals called polyphenols, which can help lower cholesterol levels. Most fruits are a good source of vitamin C, and strawberries and kiwi fruit are absolutely brimming with this vital nutrient.

Quick pumpkin and raisin cookies

75g wholemeal flour

75g plain flour

50g porridge oats

½ tsp baking powder

1tsp ground cinnamon

75g raisins or dried cranberries

100g butter, melted and cooled

75g unrefined soft brown sugar

125g cooked pumpkin purée or canned pulp

1 free-range egg, beaten

A little skimmed milk, if necessary

Makes 24

Finding healthy cookies for your children can be difficult, so why not make a batch of your own with wholesome ingredients? Perfect when you have some leftover pumpkin flesh after Halloween, otherwise use canned pulp.

1. Heat the oven to 190°C/Gas 5. In a large mixing bowl, stir together the flours, oats, baking powder, cinnamon and dried fruit.
2. In a measuring jug, beat together the cooled butter, sugar, pumpkin and egg.
3. Stir the wet ingredients into the dry, to a medium-soft dropping consistency, adding a spoonful or two of milk if necessary.
4. Drop dessertspoons, well spaced, onto a baking sheet, lined with nonstick baking paper (you may have to do this in 2 batches). Bake for 20–25 minutes until golden and firm. Cool on a wire rack until crisp. Store in an airtight tin.

Health fact: Pumpkin contains antioxidant carotenoids called cryptoxanthins, which help protect the immune system.

DRINKS AND SMOOTHIES

Just because you're eating healthily, there's no reason to miss out on delicious drinks. Many of the recipes can be halved or even quartered to serve fewer people.

Thick banana milkshake

2 large, ripe bananas, peeled and cut into chunky pieces

150ml skimmed milk

3 ice cubes

Drinking straws (optional)

Serves 4

1   Place the bananas, milk and ice in a blender. Blend on low for a few seconds, then switch to high and blend until smooth and frothy. Pour into glasses and add drinking straws, if liked. Serve immediately.

Sweet summer cooler

1 Charentais or Galia melon, halved and deseeded

250g fresh strawberries, hulled

3 ripe apricots, halved and stoned

150ml cold water

6 ice cubes

Mint leaves, to serve

Serves 4

1   Scoop the melon flesh into a blender with a dessertspoon. Add the strawberries, apricots, water and ice cubes. Blend on low for a few seconds, then switch to high and blend until smooth. Pour into 4 tall glasses. Decorate with a few mint leaves and serve.

Strawberry and banana smoothie

250g strawberries, hulled and halved

1 ripe peach or nectarine, stoned and quartered

2 bananas, peeled and cut into chunky pieces

150ml freshly squeezed orange juice

6 ice cubes

Serves 4

1   Place all the ingredients in a blender. Blend on low for a few seconds, then switch to high and blend until smooth. Pour into tall glasses and serve.

Peach and raspberry smoothie

4 ripe peaches or nectarines, stoned and roughly chopped

300g raspberries

300ml cold water

8 ice cubes

Serves 4

1   Put the peaches or nectarines, raspberries, water and ice in a blender. Blend on low for a few seconds, then switch to high and blend until smooth. Serve in slim glasses.

Kick-start smoothie

1 Stand the mangoes on a chopping board and carefully cut either side of the large, flat stone using a sharp knife. Scoop out the flesh with a dessertspoon and place in a blender.
2 Add the orange juice and bananas. Blend until smooth. Pour into 4 tall glasses and serve.

2 ripe mangoes
Freshly squeezed juice of 2 large oranges
2 bananas
Serves 4

Rainbow juice

1 Feed all the ingredients alternately through a juicer. Serve in tall glasses, over ice if liked, with extra celery sticks for stirring.

2 red peppers, deseeded and cut into thick strips
4 medium carrots, cut into thick sticks
4 celery sticks, halved
½ a cucumber, cut into thick sticks
Ice cubes and celery sticks, to serve (optional)
Serves 2–4

Spiced tomato juice

1 Feed all the ingredients, except the spring onions, alternately through a juicer. Serve in tall glasses over ice, if liked, with spring onions for stirring.

8 large, ripe tomatoes, cut into sixths
2 red peppers, deseeded and cut into wide strips
Small knob of ginger
4 celery sticks, halved
⅔ of a cucumber
Ice cubes and 4 spring onions, to serve
Serves 4

Spiced apple warmer

1 Peel, quarter and core the apples. Cut into thin slices and place in a medium saucepan with the sultanas, hazelnuts and spice. Add 300ml cold water and cook over a low heat for 10–12 minutes until softened, stirring occasionally.
2 Remove from the heat. Put the remaining cold water into the blender then carefully add the apple mixture. Blend on low for a few seconds, then switch to high and blend until smooth. Return to the pan and heat through gently, stirring occasionally.
3 Ladle into small mugs or heatproof glasses and sprinkle with a little cinnamon to decorate. Serve warm.

2 apples
50g sultanas
25g blanched hazelnuts
½ tsp ground cinnamon, plus extra to decorate
600ml water
Serves 4

INDEX

Russell Hobbs, the brand associated with quality, innovation and style in the kitchen for the last fifty years, introduces the *You Are What You Eat* product range. The range is designed to aid healthy eating by preparing and cooking food in healthier ways.

The range comprises a Quad Blade Food Processor which utilises patented four blade technology for extra speed and efficiency; Salad Xpress which slices, grates, chops and shreds vegetables, fruit, cheese and meat and dries salad in seconds; as well as a Health Grill, Steamer, Smoothie Maker and Juice Extractor. All products are designed in a crisp white finish with silver highlights and include a glossy recipe book to help get you started and assist you on the way to a much healthier lifestyle. Further products will be introduced as the range is developed.

Products are available from all major high street retailers.